LEARNING HOW TO

TRUST... *Again*

LEARNING HOW TO

TRUST... *Again*

Ed Delph, Alan Heller,
and Pauly Heller

DESTINY IMAGE® PUBLISHERS, INC.

P.O. Box 310, Shippensburg, PA 17257-0310

"Speaking to the Purposes of God for this
Generation and for the Generations to Come."

This book and all other Destiny Image, Revival Press, Mercy Place,
Fresh Bread, Destiny Image Fiction, and Treasure House books
are available at Christian bookstores and distributors worldwide.

For a U.S. bookstore nearest you, call 1-800-722-6774.
For more information on foreign distributors, call 717-532-3040.
Or reach us on the Internet: **www.destinyimage.com**

ISBN 10: 0-7684-2419-4
ISBN 13: 978-0-7684-2419-5

For Worldwide Distribution, Printed in the U.S.A.
1 2 3 4 5 6 7 8 9 10 11 / 09 08 07

Dedication

This book is dedicated to the amazingly diverse country of South Africa, a country learning how to trust all over again.

Acknowledgements

From Ed Delph

First of all, I would like to thank Jerome Dean Mahaffey, Ph.D., assistant professor of mass communication at Indiana University East. Without his and his wife Lainey's commitment to provide illustrations and writing expertise, this book would not be what it is today. Their silent, behind-the-scenes help—without which this book would have remained in the idea stage—has been invaluable. Their desire to help hurting people was my inspiration in co-writing this book.

Second, I would like to thank my wife, Becky, another silent partner who has come with me on the journey of a pastor, author, professor, and businessman. I may be the "flame thrower," but Becky is the "fuel."

Third, I would like to thank the co-authors of this book, Alan and Pauly Heller. Their experience as Christian counselors and marriage ministry experts has been invaluable in the writing of this book. This book's readers are getting the very best in Alan and Pauly.

Special thanks also to Don Milam, vice president of Destiny Image Publishers, who trusted in the leading of the Holy Spirit in publishing this book. Also, none of this would have happened without Joel Nori. Well done, Joel!

Last, but not least, I want to thank Carline Frost for her work in the editing of this book in its early stages. Carline is one of those people who makes things happen with excellence and integrity.

From Pauly Heller

My husband and I are grateful to Ed Delph for trusting us to be involved with him in this project. He is a dynamo and a visionary who never seems to run out of either words or ideas to further God's Kingdom. Ed's motivation to work on this book sent me diving into the Word and has greatly enriched my life.

I'd like to thank (along with my encourager and stabilizer, Alan) Elizabeth and Robert Benham, who allowed us to "camp out" at their vacation home, where we accomplished a substantial chunk of writing. I'd also like to thank the women in Elizabeth's Thursday morning Bible study, who have faithfully brought Alan and me before God's throne of grace, thereby giving us fortitude to stay the course and finish the book. And special thanks to Sandra Tarlen for granting us permission to publish her inspiring story.

From Alan Heller

I owe a debt of gratitude to the people who formed the foundation of my faith and trust in God: Mike Casey, Joe Webb, Rev. Paul Neal, Pastor Daryl Larson, Dr. Chris Lyon, Dr. Howard Hendricks, and the late Dr. Bill Bright. Thanks also to Stan Runnels, without whose faith and expertise we would not have trusted God to birth to the ministry of *Walk & Talk*.

To my wife, companion, lover, friend, and co-author, Pauly— thank you for undertaking this project with me.

I'm eternally grateful to God for giving us His Word, upon which I've stood steadfast for 36 years.

Endorsements

Without security (trust), relationships won't happen. For over 40 years I have been writing and counseling people on how to trust and make their relationships secure; because, with security (trust), intimacy naturally happens. Here is a book that shows you the way to regain trust and see life work. Alan, Pauly, and Ed speak from years of experience and will make a difference in your life and those you love.

> Dr. Gary Smalley
> Speaker, author of *I Promise*
> Smalley Relationship Center
> www.dnaofrelationships.com

For countless people, the idea of trust is a mirage. They've had a parent who abused them, a spouse who walked out on them, a business partner who ruined them, or a politician or pastor who betrayed their trust. Yet in order for any healthy personal or spiritual relationship to form, trust is *essential*, not optional.

So how can you learn to trust again? May I recommend this outstanding book as a wonderful tool for learning to trust again. You'll soon realize why trust is essential, and that there really are people and a God worth trusting. This book, and the biblical reality it infuses in the word *trust,* can transform your life.

John Trent, Ph.D.
Author, *The Blessing* and *The 2 Degree Difference*
President, The Center for Strong Families
Scottsdale, Arizona

Ed Delph has spent his life as a spiritual change agent and an encourager of the Believers. His worldwide influence as a preacher, prophet, and teacher is significant. In his latest book, *Learning How to Trust...Again,* he has shared deep spiritual insights and wisdom from God. I strongly endorse this book and encourage Christian servant leaders to read it.

Bishop George D. McKinney, Ph.D., D.D.
General Board Member, C.O.G.I.C.

I couldn't agree more that a lack of trust is the number one problem for many people, and maybe, especially Christians. The number two problem for those people is that they don't know how to venture out again into that dreaded arena of vulnerability and try, try again. The emotional scars that many wear are reminders of the incredible pain of betrayal in one form or another that cause withdrawal from all the basics of Christianity that Jesus taught: fellowship, love, care, gentleness, and kindness to all. This book does not merely describe persons who fail to trust, but actually shows them how to begin again, by recognizing symptoms in the "self" that point to unhealed areas and then showing them the way out.

In days gone by I spent time in the cave of self-protection and I know it's marked by loneliness and lack of fulfillment. Someone loved me enough to show me the way out and that's why I am so glad that Ed Delph wrote this book—so that others may be released in this strategic hour.

Dr. Iverna Tompkins
www.iverna.org

The inability to trust others is a problem we have run across all too often. With *Learning How to Trust...Again,* we now have a great resource to share, a resource that not only clearly spells out people's options, but walks them through the recovery process.

David and Karen Mains
Mainstay Ministries
Writers and Communicators
Originators of 50-Day Spiritual Adventures

Trust is crucial to any meaningful relationship. I am delighted to see Ed Delph and the Hellers team up to write *Learning How to Trust...Again.* This valuable resource gives lots of insight into how trust is destroyed and how it is rebuilt.

Dr. Norm Wakefield
Professor Emeritus, Phoenix Seminary

Trust is the currency of all relationships. The breakdown of trust erodes the basis of all effective functioning in family, church, or organization. Few people on the globe today have a bird's-eye view on the church and its challenges like Ed Delph. Once again, he has placed his finger on a key issue that is in dire need of being confronted so the Church can rise in effectiveness. His passion to build an overcoming Church shines through. *Learning How to Trust...Again* is a timely challenge and a must-read.

Alan Platt
Visionary Leader and author
Doxa Deo Ministries
South Africa

Ed Delph has hit another home run! This book is filled with interesting and life-changing insights; and Ed's gift of communicating is relentlessly encouraging. *Learning How to Trust...Again* will delight you and transform you.

Dr. Gary D. Kinnaman
Author and Senior Pastor, Word of Grace Church
Mesa, Arizona

This book offers hope and healing to those of us who have been hurt in the Christian life and are afraid to trust again. We believe God will use this message to help a lot of people.

Dallas and Nancy Demmitt
Counselors and authors of *Can You Hear Me Now?*
Phoenix, Arizona

Ed Delph has created the lost-and-found department for trust. An irony of trust is that one will trust his life to an unknown pilot tens of thousands of feet in the air but cannot trust those closest to him on the ground. Why? That brief question is skillfully confronted as Delph takes the reader on a journey to discover both how trust goes missing and how it is redeemed.

The hurts of life that separate people within themselves and from others—including God—are real, and they shatter trust. As a minister of inner healing, I can verify that Delph's insights and illustrations are on the mark. The title, *Learning How to Trust...Again*, speaks for itself and lures one into the book's content, which shows that reconciliation and restoration are possible. And that is good news.

Quinn Schipper
Founder, OIKOS Network Ministries
Author, *Trading Faces*

Everyone underestimates the importance of trust until it has been severely broken. Most never learn to trust again—unless they hear the message and embrace the wisdom that Ed and the Hellers describe. Every library should have this book and every person should read it.

Al Ells
Leaders That Last

Ed has done it again! In fresh and understandable language he provides profound insight from Scripture and lessons from life that bring wholeness and healing. This book is a must-read for every person who wants to grow in their "trust walk" with God.

Dr. Johan D. Engelbrecht
Founder and President, Leaders for the Nations

Over the years of my friendship with Ed, I have heard him use one of his favorite expressions, "real and tangible way," many times. Presenting the truths and principles of God in a very practical and understandable way has always been his heart's desire. Ed thinks, speaks, preaches, and writes with this basic philosophy. In this book I believe he has done it again! This book is birthed out of a pastor's heart. He can write from his life experiences—not from wounds, but rather from a position of strength and success.

Every one of us has a past filled with challenges and relationship failures of one kind or another that shape our life, define our identity, and determine our destiny—so this book is for us all! Identifying the issues of the past is the easy part, but now we have some practical tools to help us overcome these life-shaping events! Thanks, Ed!

Gary W. Carter
Senior Pastor, Drayton Valley Word of Life Centre
Drayton Valley, Alberta, Canada

If you are only going to read one book this year, it should be Dr. Ed Delph's book: *Learning How to Trust…Again*. This book will bring freedom and life to the reader who is open to the truths shared within its pages. It is a must-read.

Jeff Love
Pastor, Alive Church
Tucson, Arizona

In his latest book, *Learning How to Trust…Again*, Ed Delph presents a very clear and powerful truth that is going to help thousands regain trust and confidence and will help them experience restoration.

The lie of the devil is that God doesn't even trust His saints (see Job 15:15). But He does trust us. He knows we are all "just men and women" and we fail, but He forgives and restores, so should we forgive and forget and "Let go!" Sinners fail; saints fail; but God never fails, and He makes failures to become saints. Thank you, Ed, for this timely revelation.

Apostle Emanuele Cannistraci
Founder of Apostolic Missions International

Dr. Ed Delph has come out with a message, not just another book, on a very crucial topic: *Learning How to Trust…Again*. This is a must-read if you are in leadership for the long haul and you expect to impact your generation. What Dr. Ed is saying is what Christ said on the Cross: "Father, forgive them. I will trust them with Our work again." When those you have raised betray you, when the love of your life breaks your heart, when those you have healed and blessed hurt and curse you, the only thing you're left with is to trust again.

I have known Dr. Ed for over 20 years, and I know that he is one man whose heart and blood is in missions and in helping leaders. This book is a godsend to all of us.

Pastor Robert Kayanja
President and Founder, Miracle Center
Kampala, Uganda

ather,

We sincerely desire that You minister by the power and gentleness of Your Holy Spirit to all who read this book. Set free those who are in bondage. Let the Truth of Your Word contained within these pages penetrate even the most hardened or closed heart. Bring healing to those who earnestly seek to learn to trust You.

In Jesus' most powerful name we pray. Amen.

Table of Contents

Can I Ever Trust Again?

We all make decisions on a regular basis about whether or not to trust other people, organizations, situations, God, and even ourselves. Trust is truly one of the fundamental issues of human life. Do we trust the valet at the restaurant to park our car? Do we trust a coworker to complete an important task for us on schedule? Do we trust the driver behind us to apply his brakes in time to avoid a rear-end collision? Daily, in countless situations, we trust someone to follow societal rules or policies where our very well-being depends upon it.

But in other situations—mostly associated with relationships—many people hesitate to place trust in others. Often the stakes are high, especially with regard to hearts and emotions. Most of us have been hurt occasionally, or let down, or disappointed by people close to us and, as a result, have become prudently cautious in the degree of trust we place in others. Once in a while we run across that naive person who seems to trust everyone, and we say to ourselves, "You'll learn the hard way someday." And all too often, they do. But such is life—full of disappointment and trouble. Jesus said, *"In this life you will have trouble"* (see John 16:33), and He was not kidding.

A more serious problem arises when a person has been hurt or disappointed once too often or a little too deeply and is unable to make a normal recovery. The resultant experience takes on colossal proportions and permanently cripples the person's ability to trust others in similar situations. For example, if a woman has been hurt deeply enough, she may be traumatized into being unable to trust others in any relational situation thereafter. And, when her ability to trust becomes damaged to that degree, her likelihood of achieving a fulfilling life decreases dramatically.

This book will explain the operation of your ability to trust; illuminate precisely what goes wrong when you are deeply hurt; and prescribe the spiritual medicine that—combined with earnest prayer, courage, and the power of God—will enable you to begin to trust again. If you just can't trust other people anymore, I urge you to read this short book and lay hold of the hope that God offers you.

We would never downplay the depth of your pain nor insist that the road back to emotional health is an easy one, but there is a road and many have traveled it with no regrets. Within these pages you'll find a mixture of anecdotes, profiles, common sense and, most importantly, the Word of God. Combined they will help you understand what went wrong in your life and provide the empowerment you need to overcome what we believe is the greatest practical enemy of your emotional, physical, and spiritual well-being: the inability to trust.

—Ed Delph

—Alan and Pauly Heller

CHAPTER 1

Trust or Consequences

*"What you are willing to walk away from
determines what God will bring to you."*

—Mike Murdock

Baby Boomers may remember a popular television game show
from the 1950s–1970s called *Truth or Consequences*. Hosted by several different personalities over the years, the one I (Alan) best remember is Bob Barker. He would ask contestants to answer a trick
question. When they failed to do so, they would have to pay the consequence—a sometimes funny, sometimes embarrassing, sometimes
sentimental stunt.

This describes the way some people think God works. He's a
capricious "earth show" host who places us in unpredictable situations in which we are doomed to fail. Then He further confounds us

with difficult or embarrassing consequences—in one "no win" situation after another. How can anyone trust a God like that?

Beginning life totally dependent upon his or her parents or other adults, a baby has no choice whether or not to trust. In fact, an infant must learn *not* to trust through firsthand experience. Unfortunately, recent news reports are rife with stories of babies beaten by their mother's boyfriend or shaken to the point of brain damage by a frustrated baby-sitter. Such things ought not to be, but sadly, they happen.

However, it doesn't take such extremes for a child to learn not to trust adults. Nine-year-old Travis has a baseball game after school. His dad promises he'll be there to watch him play. But as the innings go up on the scoreboard, Travis's hopes of seeing his dad go down. Whether Dad experienced a crisis at work or stopped at a bar for a beer makes no difference. The message to Travis is the same: You can't trust Dad to keep his word.

At the age of seven, Erin already knows she's not as pretty as Angela or as smart as Amber or as fast a runner as Heather or as good at any number of things as Brittany. She's learned all these things at her after-school daycare program. Her mom says that one day soon she'll get a job that will allow her to be home when Erin gets home from school. But Mom keeps getting more promotions and more responsibility at her job, and it never happens. Erin loves her mom, but she knows she can't trust her to keep her word.

Our lives are made up of strings of fable-like circumstances—each a little story with a moral at the end. How many of your stories end with a message that says, "You can't trust him" or "You can't trust her"? As you can see from our examples, these stories don't have to be major catastrophes, though some of them are. But it doesn't take much for the message of rejection to get through to a child. By adulthood, these messages may be so much a part of the fabric of our lives that we're not even aware that our souls are cloaked in them. Yet they influence the ways in which we view ourselves, our relationships with other people, and our relationship with God.

We can view the area of trust as a road that comes to a fork. At this fork, we are faced with a decision whether to trust or not to trust, whether to try again or to operate out of our own limited resources. Of course, every day we must choose to trust others in seemingly minor issues, but the decision we're referring to here is of a more encompassing nature: Will the person standing at that fork choose a *lifestyle* of continuing to trust in spite of the disappointments, or choose a *lifestyle* of self-sufficiency based on the belief that people are generally untrustworthy? Worse yet, when a person believes that God has authored the disappointment, will he or she choose to withhold trust from Him when the stakes are high?

Where do the different forks of this road take us? Generally speaking, the fork of the "trustless" lifestyle takes us down a road that leads to a life of loneliness; for without trust, deep relationships cannot be developed and lasting relationships cannot be maintained. This road leads to mediocrity of achievement; for a person who will not trust others is limited by his or her own stock of resources and abilities—which are always less than the combined abilities of people working together. It is a road on which the enemy of our souls wants to keep us.

Ah, the "enemy." Did you know you have one? We're not making this up just to scare you. The Bible uses that very word when it says, *"Your enemy the devil prowls around like a roaring lion looking for someone to devour"* (1 Pet. 5:8 NIV). Without going into a lot of spiritual "mumbo jumbo," let's just say that if you sometimes feel as if you're being attacked, you probably are. However, the person doing the attacking is often not clothed in flesh and blood, no matter how the situation appears to you.

Scripture calls him satan, our adversary, lucifer, the serpent, the father of lies. He's the leader of a host of fallen angels who rebelled against God's sovereign rule in Heaven. He is not Jesus' brother or anywhere near His equal. But do not be mistaken; he is powerful. In fact, much more powerful than you are, if left to your own devices. Fortunately, God has not left you on your own to deal with this powerful angel of darkness. You have all the armor of God and His weapons of spiritual warfare at your disposal (see Eph. 6:10-18).

Since this book is dealing with learning to trust, and one of your primary tools in rebuilding a foundation of trust is the Truth of God's Word, let's call this enemy by one of his main attributes: liar. It is the liar who wants to keep you bound in the loneliness and mediocrity that result from lack of trust.

Without trust, your faith—the very foundation of your salvation—will erode. On the one hand, trusting provides the probability of disappointment but also the *probability of success and happiness*. But on the other, not trusting provides the *certainty of loneliness* within the *supposed safety of self-sufficiency*.

Are we saying that the lifestyle of trust is a road paved with gold and happiness? No, not always. People and things will continue to disappoint you. Your friends will let you down, forget to do promised favors, and even forget your birthday. Your husband or wife will also continue to fall short of your expectations. But by choosing to demonstrate your faith and trusting again, your life can be restored and regenerated beyond measure. Deep friendships will eventually become a reality, and achievements come much easier with the help of others.

The key step in regaining your ability to trust is to trust first in God. We repeat that because this step is absolutely critical to regaining a healthy perspective on trust, **you must learn to trust God.** Your trust in God will never, ever, disappoint you. When are able to trust God again, then it becomes possible to cautiously allow your trust to proceed into other venues. If you can develop a "vision of trust" and the blessings that are yours through trusting God, then when people let you down—and undoubtedly they will—the dream of achieving that vision strengthens and enables you to get up from that experience, dust yourself off, and try it one more time.

For me (Ed), a "vision of trust" means that no matter what happens, I have chosen to continue trusting God and trusting God's work in others. I know in my heart that God will never let me down—even though people will. God's plan for my life takes all of those disappointments into account.

Suppose that a person has experienced a business failure. Pauly's dad, Lenny, and a business partner once purchased a large building. An auto dealership occupied the entire first floor. Upstairs they remodeled a dozen or so small apartments, which they rented to residential tenants. Shortly after they replaced the roof on the building, the partner abruptly cleaned out their bank account, moved away, and took a job in another city. He left Lenny with the entire financial responsibility for their enterprise. Moreover, Lenny soon learned that his partner had not paid the roofing contractor for his work—several thousand dollars. Overnight, Lenny's financial standing changed considerably.

If you were Lenny, would the fear of another failure keep you from investing in any more real estate? I hope not. He certainly needed to know what went wrong with this man and their partnership and how to avoid such problems in the future, but to withdraw and never try again would have been a tragic waste of Lenny's business abilities. A recent poll of millionaires showed that each one had made and lost his or her million several times previously. Furthermore, it showed that the second and third million came much more quickly than the first. If those people had let fear and an inability to trust paralyze them, they would not be where they are today. As it happened, Lenny—who knew he had a terminal illness—invested in several smaller rental properties and put them into a trust to provide for his wife after his death.

Suppose that a person has had a failed marriage. Should fear of another failure keep him from marrying a second time? Certainly he should understand why the marriage failed and work on adjusting personality defects that were contributing factors. But to close himself off from intimate relationships and withdraw from meaningful friendships would destine him to a life of loneliness. Higher divorce rates in second and third marriages can be attributed to the partners' inability to trust—because their trust may have been shattered in their earlier marriage(s). Desiring companionship, people marry again and again without dealing with root issues such as lack of trust.

If you maintain a "vision of trust," you know where the forks in the road of trust lead. You embrace the choice that leads to fulfillment in life. You know that no matter how badly you are hurt, the choice not to trust will only worsen your situation. Here's an example from my own life.

In 1991, on a yearly ski trip to Taos, New Mexico, I suffered a fall on a steep hill. While sliding down the hill out of control, I recognized that something had happened but was not sure what until I finally stopped. (I hit a tree.) Then I noticed that my right leg was bent at an unusual angle. As it turns out, I had a compound fracture of the femur, an often-crippling injury. The next few weeks entailed excruciating torture while I waited for medical treatment in that small town, then had two operations to put the bones back together and began physical therapy. As I began rehabilitation, I had to choose to trust what the therapist was doing. It was painful and I did not like it. Even so, I knew that if I ever wanted to walk normally again, I had to trust in the skill of the medical experts.

Oh, how I wanted to trust that my leg knew what was best! It wanted to be left alone; it did not want to do stretching exercises. It wanted to rest instead of work. But I chose to trust the therapists, and after many months of tribulation, my leg improved and I walk normally today.

CHAPTER 2

Trust, Princess Amanda, and the Dragon

*"When you take responsibility **for** someone,
you take responsibility **from** someone."*

—Dr. Frank Freed

Imagine the limitless possibilities that would be available if you genuinely trusted God! Look at the lives of people in the Bible who trusted God. Abraham departed from his home in Ur and fathered a nation, God's holy people, Israel. Noah and his family survived the great flood and re-populated the earth. David slew Goliath. Peter walked on the water of the Sea of Galilee. The list goes on and on.

What are your dreams? What are your desires? What exploits would you like to accomplish for the Kingdom of God? What type of person do you desire to become? Are you satisfied with the process through which God is bringing you, or do you find yourself caught in complacency, mired in mediocrity, stuck, stagnant, and stifled? Many times, trust in God is the difference between the cruising or crawling Christian. The only difference between Abraham, Noah, David, Peter, and you is that those men put their trust in God. Not that they were perfect—the Bible records the mistakes and disobedience of each of them. But when everything was on the line, they trusted not in their own strength, but in God's.

Our Lives Will Rise to the Level of That in Which We Place Our Trust

If you trust in yourself, face it—you are not going to get very far. If your trust is in your superior education, you may be remembered as one who contributed to your field of study. If your trust is in idealistic ethical standards, you may be remembered as a person of integrity. But when you trust in God, anything is possible and all doors are open to you. Your life will rise to the level of that in which you place your trust.

The term "God-sized" refers to a work that is larger than human ability can manage. The key to laying hold of a God-sized task is our trust in God; as our trust level grows, so grows the mighty work He is able to accomplish through us. When David confronted Goliath, he undertook a God-sized task, which could be successfully completed only through the power of the Holy Spirit. David put his trust completely in God, and his performance rose to God's level.

David's Trust

Israel was at war with the Philistines. Two armies—perhaps 210,000 men each (see 1 Sam. 15:4)—camped on opposite sides of a valley. It was not uncommon to lose 20,000 men in a single battle in those days. Imagine David, a teenager armed with only a stick and a slingshot, having the audacity and boldness to challenge a professional soldier, the undefeated champion of the Philistines, who was twice David's size and strength. A six-year-old boy might have the same chance against an adult man. Yet David trusted in God and *knew* the God in whom he trusted.

David knew the Word of God, that God had never failed Israel in the past. He knew that God was a living God, compared to the Philistines' impotent idols—a fact that he pointed out to Goliath. Israel's God had given David victory in every prior difficult situation. David's trust was based in knowing God; it was reinforced by his experiences and sealed by his life of prayer. David knew the stakes and knew that God would cause him to prevail. David was not afraid to take the fate of his people and his country on his shoulders. His failure would have spelled disaster for Israel that day. David had already been anointed king over Israel. He trusted God's prophet and had faith that God would bring his reign to pass. He could never have been killed in this battle!

You already know that the story ended with the slight shepherd boy using his slingshot to accurately hurl a stone that hit Goliath squarely between the eyes; Goliath crashed to the ground; and David beheaded the giant with his own sword.

The same ability to lay hold of a God-sized task is available to us today, but its accomplishment is entirely dependent on the level of trust we have in God.

"Jesus looked at them [the disciples] *and said, 'With man this is impossible, but with God all things are possible'"* (Matt. 19:26 NIV). With God all things truly are possible. The great heroes of our Christian heritage have finished their race, *but God is not finished working with people.* He continues to work and desires to perform miracles in the midst of our life circumstances. He still wants to perform mighty works through anyone who will give Him the opportunity. He is longing for people who will *trust* in Him.

- Have you been rejected by another person through a divorce, causing you to give up on meaningful relationships?

- Were you snubbed by a group of church people, causing you to forsake church membership altogether?

- Have you been hurt by an insensitive pastor, and have now lost your trust in all pastors?

- Pastor, have you been hurt by an elder or by your congregation to the point of losing trust in them?

- Were you abused (physically, emotionally, or sexually) by another person, and now choose never to trust in people again?

- As a member of a minority group, have you been hurt or slighted by a ruling majority, and feel distrustful of them?

- *Do you feel that God has let you down in some way and now you cannot even trust Him, although you know in your heart you need to?*

If you feel that way and sincerely desire to learn how to trust God and other people again, then this book is for you. Reclaiming your ability to trust God is not easy. You will need to tear down some mental strongholds, let go of some dearly held conclusions about life, be willing to admit you have been wrong, and be willing to repent for not trusting God in the past. It will demand self-analysis, self-criticism, perhaps digging up some old hurts, and, most of all, *forgiveness.* Sooner or later, God will even require you to begin trusting people again. If you are serious about changing your life, then you must be willing to do these things. If you ever want to lay hold of a God-sized task, you have got to trust in God.

Princess Amanda and the Dragon

In order to learn how to trust all over again, you need to become aware of how you lose your trust in the first place. What happens to you when a shaping event in your life creates lingering influences that can affect you for the rest of your life? When a painful event occurs in your life, how does the hurt it leaves behind become an influence in the choices you make? In other words, how does a little pebble in the path of your past become a huge boulder that blocks the road to your future happiness? We want to explore the process that starts you down a road of distrust or no trust.

Dr. David and Karen Mains of Mainstay Ministries have captured this process in the first book of their Kingdom Tales Trilogy, *Tales of the Kingdom,* a children's book filled with allegorical stories about young people seeking to follow God. They have permitted us to reproduce one of those stories, "Princess Amanda and the Dragon," which describes a girl's struggle with temptation and her failure to trust in a benevolent Caretaker and his rules created for her own well-being.

This allegory may be your story. Observe how Amanda is captured by the very thing that she thinks she can tame! And think about how little offenses you hold onto can become big problems later.

"Princess Amanda and the Dragon"

Once, tall grasses grew by Lake Marmo. Each spring, damsel dragons dropped out of the sky, trampled nests in the reeds, laid clutches of eggs, and buried them in the sand. And once they had given birth, the great reptiles flapped away.

Dragons in the sky are the first sign of spring in Great Park. The children come, baskets in hand, eager for dragon-egg hunts. They shed their winter stockings and wiggle their bare toes in the warm sand. They race each other, laughing and breathless, to see who will reach a clutch of dragon eggs first. They yell and hoot when they find the treasure.

"Dragon eggs!" they cry. Soon the shout—"Dragon eggs!"—echoes back and forth from both sides of the lake.

Children know they are forbidden to keep dragon eggs, because a dragon soon hatches from the egg and it achieves full growth six months later. The baby dragon's scales harden. It begins to breathe fire. At first, there are short blasts of warm air, then later great searing torches of flame. The dragon has become cunning and cannot be trusted. So a sign on the shores of Lake Marmo reads: It Is Forbidden to Keep Dragon Eggs.

The two eggs Princess Amanda found one day many months after Hero's arrival were bronze. They glowed like amber jewels in the sunlight. Perhaps she meant to carry them to Caretaker. Perhaps she thought that they were old and shriveled inside. Perhaps she forgot. But she did not take them to Caretaker's cottage.

Instead she hid the eggs. She hid them in My Very Own Place, her den in the hollow of a mighty oak on the edge of Outpost Meadow, which was so far from Stonegate Entrance that few strangers walked to it. It was so peaceful here that Caretaker visited this area only a few times in his yearly rounds.

The spring sun reached the floor of Amanda's den and warmed her hiding place. Soon, one egg rattled when the princess picked it up to inspect it. Obviously, there was no life inside. But the other one began to crack. By midmorning a dragon hatchling pecked its way out and left the shell. The baby dragon squawked for food. Its long neck bobbed and weaved. Its feet pattered back and forth, running to keep up with its huge head. It bumped into the side of the tree. Amanda laughed.

"I must take you to Caretaker," she said aloud. "He will know what to do about surprise hatchlings."

The little beast turned its brown eye on her and a great tear dropped onto its breast. Amanda began to love the baby dragon. Though she knew it was forbidden, she kept the hatchling for a pet. *Just for a little while, she thought. Perhaps I can tame it.*

The princess fed the baby insects and wild roots. She kept it alive with hour-by-hour feedings. And because she nurtured the hatchling, she loved it all the more. The dragonet's bare skin soon became covered with soft scales, bronze and dazzling in the sun.

That summer was filled with dragonet games. The little beast and Amanda set up relay races with the butterflies. Lines of flittering wings and one sweaty princess and one growing dragonet raced through Outpost Meadow. Other days Amanda and the animal bounded over the meadow buttercups, seeing who could take the longest leap. Soon the dragonet won every time.

Sometimes Amanda tossed her ball as high as her arm could throw, and the dragonet would spring, almost to tree line, and grab it in his jaws.

"I have perfect aim. He has perfect catch. We must be a perfect match," she sang as they played in the sun.

By the middle of summer, the dragonet was large enough for Amanda to wedge herself between the spikes on its back. Together they leaped above the meadow, flying in and out of the limbs and leaves of the old trees that bordered the open field. The dragonet let out a joyous "Cree-ee-el!" and Amanda laughed with glee.

Up and down, they soared. Up high into the tree branches and down low into the flowering meadow. Amanda hung on for her life while the dragonet flew, flapping its wings.

Amanda soon discovered that her pet hated to be left by itself. It wailed piteously when she left it to perfect her aim on the practice field, so she began to practice less and less. The dragonet particularly hated to be left alone at night. Since the princess dared not bring it to Inmost Circle—and even feared for its life should it be discovered—she began to stay away from the Great Celebrations.

One night she crawled into her den beside the beast, and he licked her face and hands. Gratefully, it stretched beside her, panting with relief that she had stayed. She could hear distant music from Deepest Forest and missed her friends. Raising a hatchling was more demanding than she had thought. Amanda became angry at the law that kept her from sharing her pet with the others. *What harm is one small dragon?* she thought.

That same night she noticed a yellow gleam flickering in the beast's eyes as it looked at her. When it licked her face, she could feel that its breath was warm and dry.

After that, when Amanda returned from short trips to forage for their food, she would find the walls of her den scorched. The hollow was becoming more blackened. It smelled of charcoal. The dragon was always glad to see her, but she was careful not to stand directly in front of its nose and mouth.

More and more often, she had to be careful of its tail. A full-grown dragon's tail is deadly. Its powerful sweep can move boulders or knock down medium-sized trees or cripple a man. *Or kill a princess.*

Once, when she wanted to hop on its back for a ride, the dragon leaped up without her. "Cree-eel! Cree-eel!" Its cry became defiant as it shot a flame in her direction. For the first time, it had willfully disobeyed her.

As each week passed, Amanda began to laugh less and less.

One day, after racing the dragon through the forest, she left it napping in a sunny glade and returned to the hollow tree just as Caretaker was backing out of it. His sapling hat pulled out of the hole like a cork out of a bottle.

"What is wrong with the inside of My Very Own Place?" he asked. "Amanda, you haven't been lighting fires, have you?"

"Oh, it's been that way for a long time," she lied. "I don't know what caused that. Maybe Burners were here last winter."

Amanda wished Caretaker would stop wearing that ridiculous tree for a hat. How could she have ever thought it so wonderful!

Caretaker stared at the dirt in the front of the den. He pushed it with his foot. "Ever see any dragons around here?" he asked quietly.

"Dragons?" answered Amanda, quickly. "Now, now. The season for dragons is over."

Caretaker didn't say a word, but began to walk down Meadow Path. *You old fool*, thought Amanda. It was then that he stopped and turned and looked at her sadly.

"If you ever need me, Amanda, just call." Caretaker gazed at Amanda for several long minutes, then turned around again and went on his way.

The next day, she hid the dragon in another part of the forest. When she returned, it was Mercie who sat outside of her den. *She's the ugliest woman I've ever seen,* thought Amanda with surprise. She dreaded talking to her. *Why don't they just leave me alone?*

"Amanda!" Mercie called with a sad smile. "I saw you coming before I heard you. Whatever has happened to your laugh?"

Amanda did not know how to answer. Had she changed? Everything looked different now. Was she losing her gift of seeing? Or were things appearing now as they really were? Maybe the Great Celebration was just a bunch of foolishness.

That same night, Amanda realized that the scales of the dragon sleeping beside her were very hard. She knew that its big body was crowding My Very Own Place, and that grown dragons were no laughing matter.

This was the last night she would allow the dragon to return from its hiding place to sleep with her in the den. The next day she took it deep into the forest and commanded it to stay. Secretly, she hoped the beast would fly away. It had become too big, and Princess Amanda was afraid. Somehow, she had to get rid of the dragon. Trouble was ahead. She could feel it.

One morning a few days later she woke early. With her eyes still closed, she enjoyed the comfort of having enough room to stretch. It was a crisp fall day. She could smell the cool, dry air. And she could smell...fire! Amanda leaped to her feet. Fallen leaves had been pushed in a pile beside her hollow tree door. They were burning. Amanda rushed out, stomping and scattering. Her bare feet felt singed.

Looking up, she saw that an old stump was smoldering beside Meadow Path. Underbrush was smoking on the edge of the forest. Amanda could see something large and bronze-colored moving between the trees. She dashed in to put on her shoes and rushed back out.

"Wait! Wait!" she shouted. She began running along the path. "Wait for me!" She was terrified that the dry grass would catch fire and begin to flame from the dragon's breath. In her mind, she could see the whole forest burning, the creatures running and—oh, how awful!—fire in Great Park! Fire because of her!

Suddenly, she knew. *Great harm could come from one small tame dragon. Small tame things, grow into big wild beasts.*

Where, oh, where, was Caretaker now? Why had she not taken the hatchling to him right away? Why had she lied?

The beast finally heard her call. It stepped out of the trees into the meadow to face her. Amanda gasped. It had grown even more, and she had not noticed how much.

The huge beast sat waiting for her. Its long tail swept slowly across the ground behind it, then flicked, then swept back. The claws on one paw flexed, tearing the thatch and soil beneath it, then opened, then flexed again. A thick, wet trickle dripped out of its mouth, down its jaw. Yellow light gleamed in its eyes. The dragon had become cunning. Why had she not seen this?

Amanda drew herself to full stature. She ignored the throbbing in her feet. "Dragon," she announced in her most majestic tone, "you must go. You are too big for my den. Grown dragons are not allowed in Great Park. Your breath is too hot. Fly away!"

The dragon leered at her. It hunched, like a cat on the prowl, and moved closer and closer to her. Finally, the huge beast was near. It swept its tail, which quickly covered the distance between them. Amanda hopped over the tip. The dragon swept the long jagged tail back, faster. She hopped again. It raised its head and blew hot flame onto the grass behind her. She could hear the vegetation crackling. She could feel it beginning to burn. She turned and stamped the fire out. The dragon breathed again. More fire.

Her heart filled with terror. *One small princess cannot put out all the fires this one large dragon starts!*

The dragon breathed again. The flames licked her clothes, her hair. She slapped at the fire with her hands. She rolled on the ground. She could see the great beast inching closer, flicking its tail, the yellow light growing brighter in its eyes. Amanda backed away. She knew it was useless to run. The dragon always won the races.

"Oh help!" she cried. "Caretaker! Caretaker! I am too small for this terrible dragon. Help!"

Suddenly, she scarcely knew how, Caretaker was standing beside her. He must have come bounding the moment the flames had begun.

"Kill it! Kill it!" Amanda screamed. The great beast began to lurch. It raised itself on hind legs and roared. Flying flames filled the air.

"No, Amanda," said the old man, "I cannot kill this dragon. Only the one who loves a forbidden thing can do the slaying. You will always hate me if I do it. Only *you* can slay this dragon."

Caretaker pulled his woodsman's hatchet from the silver belt around his waist. He held it erect before him. He lifted his eyes to the sky. "In the name of the King, Amanda. For the Restoration... You must slay the dragon!"

Caretaker tossed the hatchet directly overhead. It flew high, then started to tumble down, end over end. The humming began, the singing the princess had always loved. The hatchet landed at her feet; its blade stuck firmly in the ground. Amanda reached down and firmly gripped the wood. She felt the hatchet's power as she pulled it from the soil.

By this time, Amanda had backed almost to the middle of Outpost Meadow, and Caretaker had moved out of the circle of mortal combat. Small fires were burning here and there on the grass. The princess must do this work quickly. She would only have one chance.

Suddenly, Amanda had a terrible thought. Her laughter was gone. Her seeing had disappeared. What if the gift of perfect aim had vanished as well?

The dragon was very close. She kept an eye on its tail. Though she had kept the beast alive, she knew it wanted to tear and devour her. The tail moved. Amanda leaped over it. It swept back. This time Amanda was ready. She whacked the huge tail with the hatchet. Hurrah! A long piece wiggled on the ground, oozing green dragon blood.

Perhaps there is hope, Amanda thought. *That was pretty quick aim.*

The dragon cried a terrible "Cree-ee-el! Cree-ee-el!"—not so much from pain as from rage. It reared back on its hind legs, opened its mouth, and let out a fiery blast that caught

38

Amanda full in the face. She could feel hot flames licking her hair, her clothes.

"Now, Amanda!" called Caretaker. "Now or never!"

She took careful aim, raised the hatchet, sighted the bare white patch on the breast of the weaving dragon, which was the beast's only vulnerable spot. "For the King!" she screamed. "For the Restoration!" Strength filled her arm. She let the hatchet fly.

At the same moment, the beast roared again. It caught Amanda's leg with the bleeding stump of its swishing tail. She went down onto the grass.

But Amanda's aim was true. Caretaker's hatchet hit its mark, and the great dragon came crashing down upon the little girl. Green ooze splashed over Outpost Meadow and covered the princess.

I am dying, she thought. *I will smother under this dragon's heavy body.*

Amanda felt Caretaker's hand touch her arm. Slowly, ever so slowly, the old man raised the edge of the great dragon hulk, just enough so that Amanda could inch her way along the ground to freedom.

Then Caretaker cradled the child in his arms in the middle of Outpost Meadow and wept. Amanda's hair and eyebrows and lashes were burned into crinkles. Her clothes were charred. Her face and feet were all blisters and boils and soot. She was covered with dragon's blood. She looked like an outcast.

But the Princess Amanda had won the battle. She had slain the dragon she loved.

So the princess discovered that when one loves a forbidden thing, one loses what one loves most. This truth is a hard-won battle for each who finds it and is always gained by loss.

As you read about Princess Amanda and the dragon, did you want to yell at her, "No, Amanda! Get rid of that thing before it's too late!" Or how about, "Amanda, you silly girl, can't you see that this wild beast is dangerous? Tell Caretaker the truth!"

Yet let's be truthful. Can you honestly say that there are no "dragon eggs" in your own life?

In the days when Jesus walked the earth, He sat talking with His followers. One of them asked Him, "Who is the greatest in the kingdom of Heaven?" Now why would they want to know a thing like that? Do you think they might be wondering if any of them were in the running for, say, vice president of the Kingdom of Heaven? After all, they were on the inside track, weren't they? Maybe they wanted a little clue as to how they were being ranked, how they stacked up against one another?

But Jesus deflated their egos with His reply. "Unless you change and become like little children, you won't even get through the door into the Kingdom of Heaven!"[1] That must have taken a bit of wind out of their sails. Just being buddy-buddy with Him didn't make them automatic shoo-ins, after all.

Jesus went on to say, "The world is going to hell because of the *things that cause people to sin*. These *things* are going to happen no matter what, but the man who makes them happen is really gonna pay for it."[2]

The Greek word Jesus used for "the things that cause people to sin" is *skandalizo*. It means to put a snare in the way of someone to trip him up. Did you ever see a bird trap made out of a box propped up with a stick? The stick is attached to the bait. When the bird picks up the bait, it jerks away the stick, causing the box to fall down and entrap the bird. Back in Jesus' day, that stick was called a skandalizo.

Do you get the connection? How is the stick that springs the trap like the things that cause people to sin? The temptation (the bait) sits harmlessly on the ground, until little Tweetie comes along and decides to pick it up. If Tweetie ignores the bait and just keeps bee-bopping on by, minding his own business, he'll be safe. But the second he picks up the bait, the skandalizo lets the box fall, and Tweetie's a goner.

Where was the snare, the skandalizo, for Jesus' followers? It was in their over-inflated views of themselves. They misunderstood the Master's upside-down Kingdom, where the first shall be last, and the last first. And they were ripe to get tripped up by the skandalizo of their own pride.

What was Amanda's skandalizo? Certainly, finding the dragon eggs in and of itself wasn't sinful. That sort of thing can happen to anyone, can't it? None of us can avoid coming across temptation in our path, and neither could Amanda. So she found these beautiful, jewel-like eggs. She considered taking them to Caretaker (who represents a faithful servant of God). So far, so good. But then what? She decided to *hide* them. There it is—Amanda's skandalizo.

Can you identify the circumstances, situations, attitudes, or thoughts that tend to trip you and knock you off the straight and narrow path? Let's consider for a moment what types of things can become "dragon eggs" in our lives. Certainly there are the ordinary temptations toward greed, lust, and pride. One of the New Testament writers, James, says it all begins with our own evil desires, which drag us away from God's best plan for us and entice us to sin. At every step of the way, we have a choice to let the pull of a temptation draw us further along the downward spiral toward actual wrongdoing, or to say no and reach back toward God's outstretched hand. Many sermons have been preached along these lines.

But have you ever considered that a painful circumstance from your life can become a dragon egg for you? How can pain become an evil treasure that you hoard in the deep recesses of your heart?

Take a look at the life of a modern-day Amanda—we'll call her Mandy. Mandy's father was a womanizer. By the time she was two years old, her mother had had enough of his philandering and divorced him. When Mandy was five, her mother remarried a man Mandy called "Daddy" for three years. Then Mom caught him in bed with his secretary and Daddy Number Two was out of there. By the time Mandy was 23, her Daddy Number One had remarried and divorced two more times, and her mother was on Daddy Number Four.

Mandy longs for a husband, a devoted, faithful man who will provide stability in her life. At long last she falls in love with Ray, a God-fearing man who promises to be the husband of her dreams. They marry. But Mandy hoards a dragon egg—the fear of rejection and abandonment. Every night, after saying prayers with their children, Mandy crawls into bed, kisses Ray goodnight, and retreats to the secret corner of her heart where she cradles her fear, like a multifaceted-amethyst dragon egg. She takes it out of its velvet box and strokes its enticing, deep purple edges, wondering when Ray will betray her trust and her dragon egg will hatch to reveal her darkest dread.

Now, the question is not whether or not Ray will actually be unfaithful. The question is how will Mandy respond to whatever she *perceives* as unfaithfulness.

One of life's realities is that pain is inevitable, but misery is optional. Ray will fail Mandy in one way or another. Maybe he forgets to pay the electric bill one month, and the utility calls with a reminder and a threat to cut off their power. Just an honest mistake, right? It could happen to anyone, right? Not in Mandy's secret dark corner. What if, on top of that shortcoming, Ray forgets Mandy's birthday, or their anniversary, or Valentine's Day? And he neglects to compliment her on a new hairdo or the way she's rearranged the living room furniture?

What if they have a disagreement and he raises his voice at her and it leads to a huge shouting match? What if, in her "justified" anger, she grabs a prized teacup and dashes it to the ground? "Now look what you made me do!" she snaps through a haze of tears and regrets.

But more than a teacup is broken. All these incidents serve to confirm Mandy's dragon-egg "truth": *No man can be trusted.* They will all "hurt you and desert you, and take your soul if you let them...Oh, but don't you let them." (Lyrics from "Just Call Out My Name" by Carole King.)

Whether in actual deed or simply in Mandy's imagination, her trust in Ray has been broken. But the seed of her distrust—her dragon egg, if you will—was implanted in the secret recesses of her wounded heart many years before Ray ever entered the picture.

By her repeated nightly subconscious "mantras"—*No man can be trusted...No man can be trusted*—Mandy has etched the lie that could spell the end of her marriage deeply within the structure of her soul. Poor, miserable, misled Mandy! Is there nothing she can do to reverse this destructive trend?

ENDNOTES

1. Pauly's paraphrase of Matthew 18:3.
2. Pauly's paraphrase of Matthew 18:7.

CHAPTER 3

Only You Can Prevent Dragon Fires: A Dozen Lessons From Dragon Eggs

*"Until the pain exceeds the fear,
there will be no change!"*

—Dr. Frank Freed

Yes, Mandy does possess options to reverse the direction of her life's destructive path. And the hope that exists for fictitious Mandy exists also for you.

This chapter contains several questions to help you apply dragon-egg lessons to your life. You may want to revisit these questions later in order to give them more thought.

Lesson 1: Identify Your Dragon Eggs

We'll begin with a simple—or perhaps not so simple—question: What are some dragon eggs in your life? This question will probably require you to back up a bit because today's dragons originate in the dragon eggs of our past.

Don't get stuck racking your brain for a sinister secret to answer this question. We don't want you to get hung up so early in the book. Here's my (Pauly's) off-the-top-of-my-head answer to this one:

"I think that Alan doesn't want to help me with projects around the house. My dad didn't help my mother with household projects, so I assume that Alan doesn't want to help me. And as a result, I don't ask him for help, but then I inwardly grumble about how he never wants to help me."

Can you see how my judgment of Alan is a dragon egg? Years ago, I saw that my dad didn't help around the house. I formed a negative opinion of Dad—my own version of a dragon egg. I carried that "egg" into my marriage. I saw Alan relaxing while I cleaned the house, and I watched my egg hatch. I "named" my baby dragon: "Alan Doesn't Like to Help Me Around the House." Fortunately, this dragon has not wrecked our marriage. But it certainly had the potential to do so.

Now back to you. Take a few moments and ask yourself, "What is a dragon egg in my life?"

Write your answer here:

_____

_____

_____

Lesson 2: Why Have You Hidden Your Dragon Eggs?

Why did Amanda hide her dragon eggs? Why did Adam and Eve make "clothes" out of fig leaves? Why, when they hear Mommy coming, do children hide behind their back the cookies they've stolen from the cookie jar? The answer comes in two parts: 1. They know it is wrong. 2. They fear the consequences of getting caught.

None of us was born with an innate list of all the "rights and wrongs" in the world. That would be impossible. A list identifying every potential right or wrong choice in one's life would wrap around the equator several times. (We haven't done the actual math on this, but you get the point.) None of us has advance knowledge of all the probabilities that will face us in life, nor how to identify the correct moral choice in every circumstance.

But we *can* know—and we *do* know—when we are disobeying a direct command. The immediate sense of guilt is unmistakable. That's why the cookie goes behind the back, the pilfered candy gets shoved under a pillow, the porn magazines are stashed under the mattress, and so on.

The children's book, *The Story About Ping*, by Marjorie Flack, deals with this issue on an elementary level. Ping is a duckling living with a family of Chinese "boat people" on the Yangtze River. Every day the boat master lets all his ducks out to forage on the river. Every evening he calls them back to the boat with a special "Ai yi yi" call. All the ducks know that the very last duck up the gangplank onto the boat will get swatted with a stick.

One day, Ping's head is underwater when the master calls, and he fails to respond until it's too late. He knows that he will be the last duck home and that he will receive the dreaded swat. So what does he do? He does what his fear of consequences tells him to do—he hides.

Similar situations bring out the "Ping" in all of us. Fear of discovery of our poor moral choices sends us scurrying off to our "secret hiding places," be they physical, psychological, or emotional. We tell ourselves, "If so-and-so really knew me, I wouldn't be accepted." A decision not to trust them is also a decision to never reveal that side of us to them. The longer we "live in hiding," the greater our sense of guilt and our fear of discovery.

Lesson 3: The Results of Hiding Dragon Eggs

Things always get worse. Pauly once dreamt about coming across a circle of stones about eight feet in diameter surrounding a dried-up plant. Feeling sorry for the plant, she felt compelled to water it. But her delight in seeing its shriveled leaves swell and grow quickly turned to horror. It grew too fast, becoming monstrous and threatening. She knew she had to destroy it, and she grabbed a broom and beat it back down into the ground.

Not knowing what to make of the dream, she reported it to a group of friends at a fellowship meeting. And one of them said, "The message of your dream is this: Be careful what you water." Pauly knew immediately how this interpretation applied to her. She had allowed her life to become too busy with activities that sapped her energy and emotions, and robbed her of time for more important priorities. She was becoming resentful toward Alan, who would say things like, "Have you done the grocery shopping?" or "What's for dinner?" His simple reminder of her priorities would explode like atomic guilt-bombs in her conscience.

Like Pauly, many of us coddle potentially dangerous habits. Initially we may be unaware of the threat. Daily, most men are faced with sexual temptation. Consider this: Duane sits waiting in the mall while his wife, Janelle, tries on clothes. A long-legged blond, 20-something, in a skintight sundress swishes by. At first, Duane says, "That woman is a dazzling beauty, but I'm committed to being satisfied by Janelle." That's the right response. But what happens when that dazzling beauty swishes by a second time?

Dr. Darryl DelHousaye, president of Phoenix Seminary, has said, "The first look is free. It's the second look that's the problem." Duane's second look leads to a bit of fantasy: "Hmm, I wonder what she'd be like in bed." Then a sharp mental slap on the wrist: "I can't believe I just thought that! Shame on me!" He looks around for Janelle, wondering if she can read the X-rated "thought balloon" hovering above his head. But no, she's still weighing the merits of the blue dress against the red one. Whew! He's off the hook.

Duane can rationalize his first indiscretion, telling himself, "That was just a slip-up. It won't happen again." But having dropped his guard and compromised his standards one time, the next time is just a bit easier for him. Fire didn't flash out of Heaven to consume him. And now he knows it won't. Gradually his conscience grows dull. And if the opportune situation presents itself, Duane will be ripe for a fall.

This principle applies to anything that you know you should say no to. As Christian educator D.L. Moody said, "You can't keep birds from flying overhead. But you can keep them from building nests in your hair."

Lesson 4: First Reaction to the Hatched Dragon

Coddling or incubating the dragon egg equals allowing yourself to consider the possibility of succumbing to temptation. An incubated egg holds the promise of hatching. When Amanda found the dragon eggs, she could have immediately destroyed them, but she let herself suppose that these eggs might be the exceptions to Caretaker's rule.

Likewise, when the serpent asked Eve in the Garden of Eden, "Did God really mean it when He said you couldn't eat from any tree in the garden that you want to," Eve could have walked away. She could have said, "You're a liar, and I'm not going to talk to you." But she gave herself permission to think that perhaps God didn't mean what He said. This consideration eventually led to action. She broke the one rule—the only rule—God had given her. She ate the fruit of the one tree—the only tree—of which God had said not to eat.

In that act—that eating—Eve's "egg" hatched.

What was Eve's first reaction? She was so delighted with this delicious fruit that she shared it with Adam. But Eve's second reaction matched Adam's first: a flood of guilt, a knowledge of their nakedness, an attempt at covering, a hiding from God.

What would constitute a "hatched dragon" for Mandy? Remember her *No man can be trusted* dragon egg? After five years of marriage, Ray comes home from a business trip with his clothes smelling like another woman's perfume. Later, she finds a condom in the pocket of his khakis. The perfume is actually a men's cologne he tried at a department store, he says. A coworker who failed to pick up a woman at a bar gave him the condom.

His explanations are logical, but she cannot believe them. "What do you think I am? An idiot?" she screams at him. "I knew I never should have trusted you. Everyone knows no man can be trusted." Every unanswered phone call or late arrival home reinforces the message. Soon, despite Ray's protests of innocence, Mandy is telling him, "If you think I'm such an idiot, why don't you just divorce me?" *Oh no, the "D" word.* Mandy claps her hands over her mouth. Her dragon has hatched.

What was your initial response to your own hatched dragon? Did you laugh with delight or cry with remorse? Baby sin—like any baby—is adorable, playful, cute. You may want to hug it and kiss it and tickle its plump little cheeks, and—like Eve—share your joy in it with your friends.

On the other hand, you may have immediately regretted your poor choice. You may have wished to turn back time and undo what you did. You may have shed tears of grief or kicked yourself, asking, "Oh why, oh why did I do that?" Such remorse, however, is fruitless unless it leads to repentance—a total change of heart.

Or you may have merely given up trying to fight temptation, saying, "I blew it, and there's no going back. So as long as I'm here, I might as well enjoy the darkness."

Lesson 5: Why We Love Our Dragons

The first time Gretchen got drunk, she had such fun. Her inhibitions and natural shyness vanished. She could laugh and tell stories and fit in with the crowd. She couldn't wait to do it again. But getting drunk was never so much fun again. No matter how often or how much or which alcoholic beverage she drank too much of, she couldn't quite recapture that first-time high. But she kept trying anyway.

Why do we love our dragons? Simply, we think that there will be a payoff, that the dragon will reward us with the same pleasure it promises. In C.S. Lewis's book, *The Lion, the Witch, and the Wardrobe*, Edmund meets the White Witch, who gives him some delicious Turkish Delight to eat. Tempted by the promise of more Turkish Delight, Edmund betrays his siblings and the great lion, Aslan. But the White Witch never makes good on her promise, and Edmund realizes he's been duped.

Every month, ladies' fashion magazines promise millions of women admiration, self-fulfillment, and popularity if they keep up with the latest trends. Can having a pair of $500 shoes really change your life? Especially if next month you'll need a different pair of $500 shoes?

Bradley owned a billion-dollar real-estate development company. He knew that interest rates had skyrocketed and property values had plateaued. But he lived for the adrenaline rush of developing new shopping malls and office parks. He felt worthless simply managing existing properties. Life was tasteless when he wasn't putting together deals. Something inside told him, "When you're not putting together a new deal, you're not a real man." So he kept extending and leveraging his empire. Then the bottom fell out of the market, and Bradley lost everything.

The liar tempts us with the illusion that pleasure can be extended indefinitely. Like gymnasts trying to score perfect tens, we want life to be full of tens. But the truth is that no one scores tens in every performance. Several years ago, with advances in training techniques and equipment design, many gymnasts began scoring tens rather consistently. So what happened? The judges changed the rules and raised the levels of difficulty to make the perfect ten an elusive dream once again.

Lesson 6: How We Nurture Our Dragons

Babies are helpless. They can't feed themselves, bathe themselves, dress themselves, or change their own poopy diapers. They need a caregiver for everything. But that doesn't mean they have no power. No, indeed. The shrill nature of their unrelenting cries awakens our sense of responsibility. And the satisfaction of stopping those cries with a nipple or a clean diaper or a gentle rocking to sleep reinforces our desire to nurture. When little Junior rewards us with a toothless smile or grasp of our finger, we know we're pretty terrific.

Darren has been faithfully married to Hillary for 11 years. One evening he checks his e-mail, and, uninvited, up pops the image of a seductive beauty. Darren gasps, feeling simultaneously ashamed and tantalized. Without thinking, he clicks on the proffered link and is treated to some photos that send hormones he'd forgotten he had racing through his body. His powerful response catches him by surprise. He quickly logs off the computer and leaves the room. But he can't get the pictures and the ecstatic rush out of his mind.

He's still a good husband and father, he tells himself. And he proves it to himself by lining up a baby-sitter and taking Hillary to dinner the next evening, complimenting her on her beauty and excellent attributes as a wife and mother. He makes love to her, making sure she's satisfied before he allows himself to climax. But a few nights later, when Hillary's asleep, Darren can't stop comparing their lovemaking experience with the explosive arousal he'd experienced from the Internet photos.

"Hillary knows I'm a light sleeper," he tells himself. "I often get up and check my e-mail in the middle of the night. So this is no big deal." And quietly slipping out of bed, he tiptoes out of the room to check on his new baby dragon.

How have you nurtured your baby dragon? If you avoid intimate friends, who ask what we call the "hard questions"—"How are you really?" "What has the Lord been teaching you?" "How's your thought life?"—you can keep your dragon a secret, and no one will be the wiser. Your dragon may be entirely acceptable in certain social circles, but absolutely forbidden in others. So you develop separate groups of friends, who don't know about one another. You may even keep separate cell phones, separate address books, separate e-mail accounts on separate computers.

Darren becomes so adept at compartmentalizing his pornography addiction that he is able to lie to Hillary without feeling guilty. In his mind, "that" Darren is a different person, a swashbuckling adventurer who roams the Internet seas with a dragon for a friend.

It logically follows that you will love the thing that you nurture. As you invest your time, energy, emotions, and finances in your dragon, your desire to keep it alive and protect it will grow into love. It's not true love in the romantic sense, but you lust for it because it gives you something—a sense of excitement—that you don't get out of ordinary life. Gradually, you offer less and less resistance to its allure. And when it calls, you respond because now you believe that this dragon is an essential component to your happiness in life.

Sharon can't walk past a certain coffee shop without going in and buying a triple-shot caramel-mocha-vanilla-macchiato frappa-latte with whipped cream. She can hardly afford the $50 per week she spends this way, and she's gained several pounds, but she can't stop. In fact, when she strides up to the counter to place her order, she feels confident and expectant. She believes she's part of an elite group of people who know how to order exactly what they want at this coffee-shop chain. She sees herself as sophisticated and self-assured, and it's become what Sharon considers to be an essential part of her identity.

Some women are compulsive catalog shoppers. Others can't resist the ease of bidding for items on eBay. You probably know people who spend hours chatting online with people who could be representing themselves as someone totally different from who they are. Reason and logic and concerned friends tell them to stop, but they can't give up this thing in which they've invested so much of themselves.

Lesson 7: Even Cute Baby Dragons Will Follow Their Nature

The poet Ogden Nash wrote:

> The trouble with a kitten is
> **THAT**

Eventually it becomes a
CAT.

The six-week-old, fluffy fur-ball with the big blue eyes will not remain a kitten forever. Instead of scampering and pouncing on your wiggling fingers and batting at kitty toys, it will slink and flick its tail and behave as though you didn't exist. That's the in-born cat nature of kittens. Kittens are simple to control; cats are a different story.

If sin were not pleasurable, the liar would be out of business. So he entices his intended victims with half-truths, such as, "What can be the harm of trying this one time?" "After all, who doesn't want to feel good?" "You deserve to give yourself a break." "No one is good ALL the time."

What the liar doesn't say is, "The nature of this thing is to grow big and ugly and powerful and beyond your control. Its nature is to take over your life and rob you of your former freedom and joy in the small pleasures of life. Oh, and by the way, it *will* grow to its ultimate end because that is its nature."

For more than 45 years, Siegfried Fischbacher and Roy Horn entertained audiences with their unique illusions involving jungle cats, such as cheetahs, lions, and tigers. Their Las Vegas magic show featuring these animals awed audiences for three decades. In their lavishly decorated homes, "Jungle Palace" and "Little Bavaria," their Royal White Tigers and other animals were free to roam the hallways. But one nightmarish evening in October 2003, their tiger, Montecore, gave Roy an unexpected 59th-birthday present when it grabbed him by his head and dragged him off the stage, leaving him permanently brain-injured. No one is certain exactly why the incident occurred, but one thing is sure: The tiger was behaving exactly like a tiger.

Lesson 8: First You Control It; Then It Controls You

A good example of this principle is seen in *Walk the Line,* a movie chronicling Johnny Cash's rise to stardom and his struggle with drug addiction. Cash's drug use started with a couple of pills shared by another entertainer during a road trip, and escalated until he was downing handfuls of pills at a time. At one point in the movie, under the influence of drugs and alcohol, he argued with June Carter. She refused to have anything more to do with him in his intoxicated state. Finally, staggering away, he muttered, "I'll come back when you're feeling better." Cash's "recreational" drug use had become a full-fledged addiction that robbed him of everything that mattered in his life, but he was unwilling to take personal responsibility for his misery.

Initially, our dragons appear harmless because they seem small and controllable. We seem to have power over them because we can choose to walk away at any time. Amanda thinks she and the dragon are a "perfect match" because they play so well together. Certain types of pleasurable sin make us feel "more alive." But this is a deception. Over time, the action becomes a habit and the habit becomes a necessity. During this transitional phase, pride and denial enter the picture. We're losing control and need help, but we don't want to admit it. Friends may notice changes in our behavior. But rather than admit the possibility that they are right, we begin isolating ourselves from those friends. Having begun with a lie, such as "I can stop doing this any time I want to," we have trouble admitting the truth: "This thing has gotten out of my control. I need help."

So we continue feeding ourselves lies such as: "Other people may have trouble with this thing (this habit, this drug use, this anger problem, this illicit behavior), but not me. I'm different." We consider ourselves to be the exceptions to the rules, somehow above the laws of human behavior that govern every other person in the universe.

At the same time, we underestimate the dragon's increasing strength. We continue to view it as controllable long after it has gained a life and power of its own. Back in the days of vinyl records, the folk-singing Smothers Brothers recorded a song about the "Slitheree Dee." It went something like this:

Oh the slitheree-dee,
it crept out of the sea,
you may catch all the others
but you won't catch me.

No you won't get me,
you old slitheree-dee,
you may get all the others,
but — GAKcckkk!

Lesson 9: We Reject the Law That Protects Us

Laws exist to maintain order in society. Without traffic laws, our streets would be chaotic and dangerous. Without civil law, gangs and guns would rule our cities and towns. Laws protect us from the natural tendency toward selfishness that is inherent in every person. The same holds true for moral law. The simple tenets of God's Ten Commandments speak to the basic motives and needs within everyone's heart: Our need for order and a final authority is addressed—"worship the one true God"; our need to earn a living—"work six days a week"; our need for rest and refreshment—"keep the Sabbath"; our quest for self-gratification at others' expense—"don't murder, steal, commit adultery," and so on.

Are these laws on God's books to make us unhappy? Absolutely not. Our Creator God, who knows best what we need to function optimally, loves us. And He prescribed simple guidelines for the greatest good of all people.

A parent tells a child, "Don't touch the hot stove" or "Don't run out into the street without looking both ways." Is that parent trying to make the child's life miserable? Of course not. Parents want to protect their child from the danger they know exists by experience.

Amanda *knows* she should take the baby dragon to Caretaker, but she *chooses* not to, in direct violation of Caretaker's posted warning: It Is Forbidden to Keep Dragon Eggs. She *doesn't forget* the law. She actively decides not to follow it.

Perhaps I can tame it, she thinks. In rationalizing her actions, she rejects the law that was drafted for her own well-being.

Have you ever exceeded the speed limit? What do you say to yourself as you drive along ten miles per hour (or more) above the posted speed? "That's a stupid law. I don't have to obey it. No one else is going that slowly. I'll look like an idiot if I hold to that speed. Other drivers will honk their horns at me. That law is for bad drivers, not for experienced drivers like me." In his seminar "Laugh Your Way to a Better Marriage," Mark Gungor remarks about speed limits. If the posted speed limit going around a sharp curve is 40 miles per hour, and you're going 70 miles per hour, he says, "It doesn't matter if you're playing Christian music—you're still going to go off the road."

In the course of rejecting the law, we also reject the authority who gives us the law. When confronted with evidence that she's hiding a dragon, Amanda denies it. She lies to the people who care about her. In trying to protect herself and her harbored sin, she swaps the definitions of good and evil. So in her mind the truth becomes a lie, and the lie becomes truth. And in so doing, she rejects the Caretaker who has only her best interests at heart. She begins to characterize him and his representatives as ridiculous and outdated, unappealing and ugly. She turns down their offers of help, denying that she needs it. She starts to slide down the slippery slope from skepticism to disrespect to rejection to mockery.

This pattern of rationalization and rejection occurs in us, too, as we lose trust in God's goodness and start characterizing Him as a huge party pooper in the sky who just doesn't want us to have any fun in life. When we're keeping His law, we agree that it's a good law. But if, after breaking the law, we rationalize our actions, then our attitude toward Him changes to realign with our self-serving, distorted view.

The more we believe the liar's lies, the less we desire to read or hear God's Word. The Truth that sets us free from sin feels like shackles to an impossible standard instead. "This is too hard!" we cry. "What does He expect of me? He's a cruel taskmaster. He never wants me to have any fun." The liar wants us to feel this way and does whatever he can to propagate these misconceptions. If we believe that God is vindictive and takes delight in punishing us, then why would we want to return to Him?

Lesson 10: When You Call for Help, the Lord Is There

Eventually, we, like Amanda, realize that this thing has gotten beyond our control. With that realization comes a feeling of hopelessness. We don't think we can ever be forgiven, or that we'll be able to change. We lapse into self-pity or self-loathing or self-destruction. Certain events may have traumatized our lives as children, but we were helpless and didn't know how to deal with them at the time. However, now we're adults, yet still feel helpless because we don't have the knowledge or the will to turn our thinking around.

Yet as soon as Amanda cries out for Caretaker, she finds him standing beside her. One moment she is all alone facing insurmountable odds; the next moment her only hope for salvation appears at her side.

Psalm 46:1 says, *"God is our refuge and strength, a very present help in trouble."* One of God's attributes is *omnipresence.* In other words, God is always present. He is eternally present. He is *everywhere* present. He is *never not* present. But we are not always aware of His presence. And at times—like Adam and Eve in the garden—we want to undertake the impossible task of hiding from His presence.

After He was raised from the dead, Jesus appeared to His disciples and gave them instructions to go out into the world and teach people about Him. Then He said, *"I am with you always, even to the end of the age"* (Matt. 28:20). Today—2,000 years later—that promise still holds true. Jesus, the living Son of the living God, is with us at all times.

Several years ago, Pauly was involved in a car accident. Although the front end of her car was sheared off, she felt shaken but uninjured. A well-meaning bystander called 911, and Pauly soon found herself on a gurney in an ambulance that whisked her to a nearby emergency room. In spite of Pauly's protests that she felt fine, a nurse immobilized her head inside a huge plastic collar, strapped her arms and legs to a table, and walked out of the room.

Five minutes went by. As Pauly lay helpless on the table, the shock of what had transpired hit her and she began to feel nauseous. Then she realized that she was unable to turn her head, and if she vomited, the consequences could be disastrous. The more she thought about this ghastly idea, the more convinced she became that she was going to throw up and aspirate and die and no one would even know. A feeling of panic enveloped her and she tried to call for the nurse, but her mouth and her mind felt like they were filled with cotton gauze. In desperation, she thickly muttered, "Jesus, help me!"

Within seconds, peace replaced panic as the Lord's calming presence filled the room. The nausea passed. She found her voice and cried, "Nurse!" Moments later, help arrived in the form of a nurse who undid the collar and released Pauly's arms and legs so she was free to move once more.

Lesson 11: Only You Can Slay Your Dragon

Amanda screams at Caretaker, "Kill it! Kill it!" But Caretaker wisely refuses. He tells her, "Only the one who loves a forbidden thing can do the slaying. You will always hate me if I do it. Only *you* can slay this dragon."

At her weakest point, when she feels least able to control the dragon and most hopeless about her situation, Amanda is told that she needs to take responsibility for putting to death the thing that has entrapped her. Just as a diet program will not work until the person who needs to lose weight chooses to do it for him- or herself, and an alcoholic will not attain sobriety if it's only to please another person, so the motivation to be free of our dragons must come from within us.

As much as Mandy wants to blame Ray for their impending divorce, she must recognize her contributions to their situation. If this relationship goes "down the tubes," she will carry her dragon song, *No man can be trusted,* into all her future relationships. Ray pleads with her, for the sake of their children, to see a counselor.

After several visits and much painful soul-searching, Mandy recognizes her dragon for the first time. Abandoned by one "Daddy" after another, and sure that her children's Daddy will do the same to her and to them, she's been blind to Ray's faithfulness as a husband and father. A week before their divorce will be final, Mandy sobs in her counselor's office. "Please tell Ray how wrong I've been. I want to start over."

"No, Mandy, you need to tell him yourself. This is a job that no one can do for you. And you need to apologize to your children for implying that their father is untrustworthy," her counselor replies.

"But he'll hate me! My children will hate me!"

"Mandy, those are risks you'll have to take. Do you want to perpetuate the pain you've experienced in your children's lives?"

"No, of course not."

"Then you must put this lie to death."

Lesson 12: You Will Not Escape Unscathed

Even though Amanda kills her dragon, the walls of her den are still scorched and blackened. For the rest of her life, her face and feet will bear the scars of burns. Others who inhabit the now-charred forest and meadows, as well, will live with the results of her irresponsible behavior.

Jesus tells the story of a young man who leaves home with all his inheritance money and quickly blows it on empty pleasures. Starving and poverty-stricken, he makes his way back home to beg his dad to hire him just so he can eat. But his father does far more. He welcomes his son home with a grand celebration. However, the fact remains: The young man's inheritance is gone. He has a place to live as his father's son, but no more money will come his way. His dragon is dead, but he must still face the consequences of his actions.

Blake was raised on a farm in Nebraska where his parents lived until, following his father's death, his mother suffered health problems and had to move in with his sister in California. Blake was between menial jobs in Vail, Colorado, where he had gone to seek his fortune as a professional skier, when his sister, Dolores, called him.

"Blake, please come home and take over the farm," she said. "No one else cares about our land. If you don't do it, I'll have to sell everything to pay off the bank loans."

But Blake refused to put his grandiose ski plans on hold, and Dolores was forced to liquidate their property. Two years later, after tearing cartilage in both knees, Blake's skiing "career" skidded to a halt. He called Dolores.

"Dolores, I'm so sorry. I realize now that I was wrong not to take over the farm. Please forgive me."

"Sure, Blake. It's OK. That was your decision. Mama and I forgave you long ago."

"But I'm out of money. I can't ski. I'll never get ahead working as a waiter. I'm in debt up to my ears. I'm kicking myself now. How could I have been so stupid?"

"Well, Blake," said his sister matter-of-factly, "you can't cry over spilled milk. So just get on with your life."

Like the prodigal son and Blake, we must make decisions about our dragons. The longer we put off dealing with them, the more serious the consequences become, and the more of our future happiness we squander.

Fortunately, our society offers a variety of resources to help restore us to health following our dragon battles. Programs such as Celebrate Recovery™, Cleansing Stream™, and 12-step groups provide supportive forums for healing intervention in our lives. Others who have dealt with similar issues come alongside those who are just beginning their journey toward wholeness.

The movie *Walk the Line* depicts a childhood incident in which Johnny Cash's older brother dies as the result of a sawmill accident while Johnny is out fishing. Their alcoholic father blames young Johnny, saying, "Where were you?" Throughout his life, Johnny bears the emotional pain of this incident and can't shake the thought that the wrong son—the good son, who was going to be a preacher—died. Many years later his father boasts that he's been sober for some time. He has slain his alcoholic dragon. Yet, despite Johnny's musical successes, his life has been irreversibly damaged by his father's rejection. At a turning point in Johnny's life, he confronts his father saying, "Where were *you*?" Soon after, he confronts his drug addiction and kills his dragon. But he bears emotional scars for the rest of his life.

Quick Review

By way of review, here are your 12 lessons from dragon eggs:

LESSON 1:   Identify Your Dragon Eggs

LESSON 2:   Why Have You Hidden Your Dragon Eggs?

LESSON 3:   The Results of Hiding Dragon Eggs

LESSON 4:   First Reaction to the Hatched Dragon

LESSON 5:   Why We Love Our Dragons

LESSON 6:   How We Nurture Our Dragons

LESSON 7:   Even Cute Baby Dragons Will Follow Their Nature

LESSON 8:   First You Control It; Then It Controls You

LESSON 9:   We Reject the Law That Protects Us

LESSON 10: When You Call for Help, the Lord Is There

LESSON 11: Only You Can Slay Your Dragon

LESSON 12: You Will Not Escape Unscathed

CHAPTER 4

"Shaping Events" and Lingering Influences

"God made lucifer, but a process made satan."

—Unknown

◆•►◦▓◦◄•◆

Have you noticed in your life that "stuff" happens? If you live long enough, you'll observe that the dawn of every day does not necessarily hold wonderfully joyous experiences in store. Maybe the marriage you thought would last for a lifetime ended up disintegrating. You knew that divorce happens but never thought it would happen to you. You may be a pastor who thought the church you serve would never ask you to leave. Or perhaps you've always been the "healthy" one, and now a potentially terminal illness has you in its grip. You thought your family seemed so perfect, yet one of your children attempts suicide. Your father, whom you trusted so fully, turns out to be an alcoholic. You trusted the company for whom you worked faithfully throughout your career to honor its pension fund commitments, and now they've declared bankruptcy. Get the message? Life happens and "stuff" happens in life.

No Pain...No Pain

The Bible says, *"For He causes His sun to rise on the evil and the good, and sends rain on the righteous and the unrighteous"* (Matt. 5:45). Elsewhere it says, *"Where no oxen are, the trough is clean; but much increase comes by the strength of an ox"* (Prov. 14:4 NKJV). In other words, "Manure happens." Where there is life, there is manure. However, much more good than bad comes out of a hardworking ox. In fact, if the manger is clean, there is no life at all. Graveyards are clean because there is *no life* there. So, both good and not-so-good things will happen in life. The key is what we *do* with both the good and the not-so-good things that happen to us. Sometimes the not-so-good things may be our fault, or may be partially our fault, or may not be our fault at all. Nonetheless, it's what we do with and how we react to these life-shaping events that determine our quality of life.

Pain in life is inevitable, but *misery is optional*. It's possible to be rejected but not affected. When a negative "shaping event" occurs in your life, you can appropriate emotional intelligence to guide you through the storm. In other words, you need to appreciate and acknowledge your emotions but use them in an intelligent manner to give you the best possible chance of success. Emotions are wonderful servants, but terrible masters. Emotional intelligence is like a rudder on a ship. It navigates you through the storm to safer seas and harbors. "Storms" happen, but also "calm" happens! The key is to go through the storms and not lose your bearings in the midst of the storm. God wants us to get our direction from Him, not from the past.

Remember, most people expect to live their life by a "no pain...no pain" type of philosophy. But as is true in so much of the sporting world, the truth is: "no pain...no gain."

Destiny Determiners

What I (Ed) call "shaping events" are those things that occur in our lives that have significant power to either make us or break us. Shaping events are destiny determiners. Shaping events are destiny definers, and they set on fire the course of our lives, either positively or negatively. A positive shaping event may propel us to a new job, a new profession, or a new chapter in our lives. Our first new car, our first promotion, and our first successful investment can be catalysts or launching pads that create beneficial effects in our lives for years. Other examples: meeting the right person, getting a break at the right place at the right time, or investing in Microsoft Windows in the early 1990s.

Negative shaping events could be a divorce, a betrayal, a disappointment, or a tragedy. These types of shaping events may create negative lingering effects for years, even your entire lifetime. The lingering effects of the World Trade Center tragedy will influence the United States for decades—perhaps forever.

Shaping events result in lingering influences. Many people in the general public relate to the Twin Towers incident on a personal level. They feel as if someone drove two jetliners into the "Twin Towers" of their life. As on September 11, 2001, such people can cite the day when life all came tumbling down. And just as many others—rescuers and innocent bystanders and shocked surviving family members—were hurt or killed with them. That's what this book is about—getting you through the lingering influences and back on the road to trusting again, warning you not to take the dragon egg of not trusting again into your version of "My Very Own Place." We want to help you slay the dragon of distrust if it has grown due to your own nurturing. Only you can prevent dragon fires!

Self-Fulfilling Prophecies

To repair and regain your damaged trust, you need to know how the process works whereby shaping events create lingering influences. Let's look at a story in the Bible. It's a sad story that Jesus told of a man who holds an entirely wrong picture of God. Certain lingering influences created that picture in his mind and emotions. Subsequently, that wrong picture of God shaped his destiny. But where did it come from? Read on:

For it is just like a man about to go on a journey, who called his own slaves and entrusted his possessions to them. To one he gave five talents, to another, two, and to another, one, each according to his own ability; and he went on his journey. Immediately the one who had received the five talents went and traded with them, and gained five more talents. In the same manner the one who had received the two talents gained two more. But he who received the one talent went away, and dug a hole in the ground and hid his master's money.

Now after a long time the master of those slaves came and settled accounts with them. The one who had received the five talents came up and brought five more talents, saying, "Master, you entrusted five talents to me. See, I have gained five more talents."

His master said to him, "Well done, good and faithful slave. You were faithful with a few things, I will put you in charge of many things; enter into the joy of your master."

Also the one who had received the two talents came up and said, "Master, you entrusted two talents to me. See, I have gained two more talents." His master said to him, "Well done, good and faithful slave. You were faithful with a few things, I will put you in charge of many things; enter into the joy of your master."

And the one also who had received the one talent came up and said, "Master, I knew you to be a hard man, reaping where you did not sow and gathering where you scattered no seed. And I was afraid, and went away and hid your talent in the ground. See, you have what is yours."

But his master answered and said to him, "You wicked, lazy slave, you knew that I reap where I did not sow and gather where I scattered no seed. Then you ought to have put my money in the bank, and on my arrival I would have received my money back with interest. Therefore take away the talent from him, and give it to the one who has the ten talents." For to everyone who has, more shall be given, and he will have an abundance; but from the one who does not have, even what he does have shall be taken away (Matthew 25:14-29).

In this story the master represents God. The slaves are God's people, the nation of Israel. Notice, the slave called God, "a hard man, reaping where you do not sow and gathering where you scattered no seed." The result of his definition of God was "and I was afraid and went away." There it is—*fear and rejection of God*—because of a wrong definition of God. The wicked, lazy slave said, "I knew you to be a *hard man*."

In His Own Image

What a tragedy! Here is someone *born to win*, but *conditioned to lose*. He lived a self-fulfilling prophecy concocted in his own mind. The Bible tells us that God is good (see Ps. 136:1). God gave him the privileges of life, talents, abilities, opportunities, eternal life, money, a livelihood, and living quarters, but out of his fear, this well-cared-for slave saw God only as "a hard man." He "knew" God to be a hard man. See that? You can have a misconception and think that you "know God to be a _____," but not really know God at all. God is not mean. God is not hard. God is good. God is generous. God was *for* this slave, not against him.

Where did this man get this theology of "reaping where you do not sow and gathering where you scattered no seed"? Where did that come from? After the great flood of Noah, God promised, *"As long as the earth endures, seedtime and harvest...will never cease"* (Gen. 8:22 NIV). In other words, you can only reap and gather where you have previously sown. You can't have a harvest without sowing any seed, yet this man "knew" God, knew that God demanded a reaping where nothing was sown. That would make any of us fearful, too! We would feel rejected, too. And that would certainly isolate us and make us feel hopeless as well.

Jesus pitied the man. The man had redefined God and made Him after his own image. He lived out the self-fulfilling prophecy he had concocted. Jesus said "OK, have it your way—I won't make your choices for you. But I didn't choose your destiny—you did—but that's not what I wanted for you." Ouch! God will not violate our right of choice. That's what being made in the image of God is all about. We have a choice. That's both good news and bad news, isn't it? If it's going to be, it starts with me!

What Was It?

What was the "shaping event" in the slave's life that started him on the road to the "lingering effects" of fear, distrust, rejection, and isolation? What caused that? Was it something in his childhood? Was his father not a good representation of God to him? Or was it an unrelated event for which he held God responsible? Did he judge God for some disappointment or disillusionment in his life? What was it?

I'm not going to get into the theology of God and His dealings with Israel. Suffice it to say that in this case, it started a long time ago. That's true with many of us. Our lingering effects started long ago. But now it's time to move from the past to the present. Yesterday's "if onlys" and tomorrow's "what ifs" prevent us from enjoying today's "what is."

So what was *your* shaping event? Where did you pick up your dragon egg?

What starts the process within a beautiful girl who looks into a mirror and thinks she's overweight when she's not? Where does that lie originate? How does it develop into bulimia? What is the process?

Where did the shaping event originate that has now grown into the dragon of drug addiction, sexual addiction, or a gambling addiction?

What initiated a handsome man's inability to commit to a long-term relationship? How about the professional football player who has it all and squanders it all and ends up selling used cars? What would cause the popular pastor of a thriving megachurch to fall for his secretary and lose everything and everyone dear to him in the process? What is it?

Why is it? Why does a Nazirite like Samson have the strength to defeat great enemies, yet he can't control his sexual desires? Why does a Delilah have such power over him? What turned an anointed King Saul into a consulter of witches? What disqualified Nazareth so that Jesus could do only a few small miracles in His own home-town? What shaping event caused Jesus to say of them, "A prophet is not honored in his own city"? What derailed unlimited potential and kept it in the realm of unfulfilled reality?

The answer to all these questions is simple yet complex. The answer is "dragon eggs." Shiny, enticing dragon eggs that we pick up when we know we shouldn't—forbidden dragon eggs that we take into "My Very Own Place." Little dragon eggs that grow into big, fire-breathing dragons living off the confusion they create—in your mind, will, and emotions.

All Men Are _____. All Women Are _____.

Around 600 B.C., the Cretan philosopher Epimenides wrote a poem titled "Cretica," where he proclaimed: "The Cretans, always liars, evil beasts, idle bellies!"[1] Did he mean every Cretan ever born or ever to be born—including himself—is a liar? If so, how can we trust *him* to be telling the truth? Did he mean that among the entire population of an island, not one person was at least halfway honest? Were Cretans always "evil beasts"? Were all Cretans "idle bellies" (lazy gluttons)? How did anyone ever get anything done on Crete if everyone was lazy? Was there not one thin person on Crete? Get the message?

This kind of generalizing is absurd. However, we do it all the time. "All men are _____." All women are _____." "All churches are

_____." "All liberals are _____." "All conservatives are _____." "All politicians are _____."

Hurt people tend to hurt people. They categorize, judge, generalize, and rationalize. They believe in lies that seem rational to them.

The truth is some men *are* ____, but not all men. Some women are ____, but not all women. Some Cretans were ____, but not all Cretans. You fill in the blank.

Perhaps you have been seduced by the dragon of overgeneralization. This dragon exaggerates and dominates by making a single event in your life the template for every other event in your life. We will discuss overgeneralization in more detail in Chapter 7.

Choose to Be Teachable, Not Offended

Offended people are easily hurt. They act out. Often they are unteachable or unforgiving or both. When you live your life like that, you become a "magnet for calamity." You become like a lightning rod, attracting all kinds of unwanted chaos into your life. Your past can be a problem or your past can be a teacher. Either way, it is the prophet of your future.

One definition of maturity is "taking the opportunity to come through an experience of disappointment or disillusionment without becoming wounded, bitter, or cynical." This book is about the "whats" and "whys" of trusting. It is also going to teach you how to come through that time or experience of disappointment or disillusionment in one piece. If you will let it, this book will "get your motor running" again—without your becoming wounded, bitter, or cynical. We want you to be pure again. Remember, to the pure, all things are pure. Conversely, to the defiled, everything is defiled (see Titus 1:15). It's a choice.

Root...Shoot...Fruit!

Did you know that the Bible has a perfect example of a dragon egg story? Look at Hebrews 12:15-17:

See to it that no one comes short of the grace of God; that no root of bitterness springing up causes trouble, and by it many be defiled; that there be no immoral or godless person like Esau, who sold his own birthright for a single meal. For you know that even afterwards, when he desired to inherit the blessing, he was rejected, for he found no place for repentance, though he sought for it with tears.

This passage refers to a "root" of bitterness. Roots of bitterness "spring up" and cause all kinds of trouble. Roots grow into shoots and produce fruits—either good or bad. Good roots of love, peace, and forgiveness produce shoots and fruits of blessing. However, in Esau's case, the focus is a root of bitterness. The firstborn of twin sons, Esau was his father's favorite. So assured was he of his father's favor that he disregarded the spiritual value of his birthright and sold it to his younger twin, Jacob. Later, Jacob tricked their father into giving him the coveted blessing his father meant for Esau. And it was permanent—no turning back. Number One Son had become Number Two. Then Esau fell victim to rejection; his heart became so embittered that he couldn't repent or even ask for forgiveness. He couldn't forget, forgive, or move on even in the midst of his tears. Whether right or wrong, he didn't get what he wanted, and it was killing him. The dragon of bitterness grew huge and enslaved Esau for the rest of his life—and for the lives of generations of his descendants. Jacob's clan became the nation of Israel; Esau's numerous offspring became the Edomites, but have entirely disappeared as a separate people today.

Where did Esau's problem start? With a prideful, impulsive decision that resulted in a mistake he thought he could handle. But the root became the shoot that produced bad fruit. It reminds me of lines from a Trini Lopez, 1960s-era, folk-rock song that compares love to sweet-smelling, though sour, lemons: "Lemon tree, very pretty, and the lemon flower is sweet, but the fruit of the lemon is impossible to eat."

Like Amanda's dragon story, Esau's example demonstrates that little things turn into big things that become untamable.

God Made lucifer, But a Process Made satan

Shaping events can cause lingering effects that have the power to paralyze us. The slave in Jesus' story may have had unmet expectations of his master (God). Perhaps God didn't act the way the slave thought He would. I imagine him saying, "If God is so good and loving, why did He let this happen to me?" Or maybe he was offended by a rabbi or other synagogue official. Maybe he, like Esau, was embittered by sibling-rivalry issues. No matter what instigated his judgmental misconception of God, you can be sure that the issue that made him stumble was not dealt with properly. He never took his "egg" of offense to Caretaker. That egg hatched; the hatchling grew and became untamable. It started with a root, became a shoot, and produced fruit—the fruit of bitterness.

A similar process transformed lucifer into satan. The Bible says lucifer was the chief musician in Heaven. God created him to be the choir director of Heaven! He was created to be the crème de la crème of the angels in Heaven. He was created to hold the highest position in Heaven besides the Father, Son, and Holy Spirit. But a little dragon egg of pride began to hatch in lucifer's mind. Rather than be satisfied with his position in Heaven, he wanted to be God. The choir director wanted to be the head pastor. His pride of face, grace, and place hatched, grew, and dominated him. Lucifer became satan. The world has been paying for his pride ever since.

Where did it start? In a little place in his mind. As a result, Heaven had its own version of a "church split" long before there was such a thing as a church. In fact, satan was kicked out of Heaven to fall to earth. He took one-third of that "church"—comprised of angels—with him.

Even God went through a church split!

Only You Can Prevent Dragon Fires

If it's going to be, it starts with me! This is an important principle. I assure you, God is ready for you to live the rest of your life. Are *you* ready?

Remember when Caretaker told Princess Amanda that she must slay her dragon. He would provide the weapon, but she needed to use it. Similarly, only you can slay the dragon you love. *If Jesus were to slay your dragon before you were ready, you would hate Him for it.* Jesus will not violate your will. You are made in the image of God. Consequently, you have a choice. You can trust in God or stay where you are. So take aim with the "hatchet" He gives you and let it fly.

You see, *having* a weapon called trust and *using* it are two different things. The truth is, when you take responsibility *for* someone, you take responsibility *from* someone. In his book *Wisdom for Crisis Times*, author Mike Murdock demonstrates his gift of one-liners. Following are a few that capture the "responsibility factor" required for a person to get back on the road to learning how to trust all over again:

- Those who created yesterday's pain do not control tomorrow's potential.

- Whatever you can tolerate, you can't change.

- What you are willing to walk away from determines what God will bring you to.

- Sometimes you have to do something you hate to get to something you love.

- Stop looking at what you can see and start looking at what you can have.

- Misery is a yesterday person trying to get along with a tomorrow God.

- When you let go of what is in your hand, God will let go of what is in His hand.

- The smallest step in the right direction always creates joy.

- The broken become masters at mending.[2]

The basic problem is that most people are doing nothing about the basic problem. But that's not you, or you wouldn't be reading this book. You want to get better. You want to grow. You want to live up to your potential.

Remember the principle: *If it's going to be, it starts with me.* Do *your* part so that God can do *His* part. You've got to learn to handle your problems or your problems will handle you. Are you ready? Let's apply principles from dragon eggs to the issue of trust.

ENDNOTES

1. http://en.wikipedia.org/wiki/Epimenides.

2. All quotes, except the fourth one, are from Mike Murdock, *Wisdom for Crisis Times* (Tulsa, OK: Honor Books, 1994), in order of appearance, 51, 93, 6, 54, 52, 32, 5, 66. Fourth quote from Mike Murdock, *One-Minute Businessman's Devotional* (Tulsa, OK: Honor Books, 1992), 37.

CHAPTER 5

Trust — The Key That Starts the Car

"Gentlemen, we are surrounded by
insurmountable opportunities!"

—Unknown

◆━▸◈◂━◆

Imagine that you own a car with a stunning exterior finish, a luxurious interior, a computer-controlled ignition and fuel system, satellite mapping capability, cruise control, a cutting-edge sound system, an incredibly powerful engine, the best tires, and four-wheel drive. Yes, it looks nice, but it won't go anywhere if you don't have the key.

Your life is like that car. You may be intelligent, have a good education, have an interesting personality, be energetic, and possess everything else the world says will make you successful. But if you have lost your ability to trust, then you are like that car without the key.[1] The keys to that car come at a cost—either a lot of money up front or a lengthy commitment to pay as you go. Likewise, trust is no easy thing to acquire once you have lost it.

What Makes Trust in God Difficult?

For most of us, trust in God is difficult because of three forces that work against every believer: the world, the carnal nature, and our enemy, the liar. Not only are these forces at work against your ability to trust but against every other aspect of your life as a child of God.

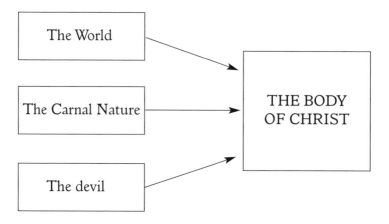

Three forces that exert pressure on Christians to conform to the Kingdom of Darkness.

1. The World

The motto "In God We Trust" appears on American coins and currency, yet few Americans indeed trust in God. What has changed our nation's society so much in the past century that we no longer want to proudly proclaim our trust in God? Why have we drifted so far away from our godly heritage?

In 1776, the United States of America was birthed by the Declaration of Independence. Since then, the idea of an American as a self-sufficient, self-reliant, rugged individualist has become a stronghold in our thinking. Such strongholds have "exalted themselves against the knowledge of God," presenting formidable roadblocks to people yearning for the life of Christ.

Today, our culture, its media, and its icons tell us, "Don't trust anybody" and "Do your own thing." Daily inundations from a giga-byte of sources teach our youth to be wary of adults and all other authority and to rely strictly on themselves and their equally skepti-cal peers. Individualism has saturated this culture. Many of us don't even know our neighbors.

As you go through your day, be on guard for the subtle rhetoric that would persuade you to be self-reliant. As a part of the Body of Christ, you are to be bonded to God and other brothers and sisters in the faith. If you are one of those believers who float from church to church without becoming part of the community that exists within a local body, then spend some time alone with God, ask Him where you should be "planted," and begin to sink your roots into meaningful relationships with others in that fellowship.

We will touch more on this issue later, but now we need to focus on the other two forces.

2. The Carnal Nature

In the area of trust, our carnal nature—the Bible calls it "the flesh"—usually works against us. Our flesh wants to satisfy itself and its appetites. So it is by nature resistant to any authority. Therefore, our flesh tells us to trust in ourselves. We've all experienced hurts, re-jections, and disappointments when our trust has been violated. The natural response to the pain of these experiences is to not trust. Self-reliance feeds our egos. It makes us feel good and gives us a sense of power after we have been hurt and let down by others.

3. The devil

All three of these forces are intertwined, but the intelligence that makes them work in harmony against us is our enemy, satan, to whom we refer as the liar.[2] As the book progresses, we will examine a specific strategy of the liar that attacks our ability to trust, and how that particular strategy fits into the liar's global strategy against mankind in general.

All of this puts you in a tough position. These issues render it difficult to trust God, but Jesus commanded you to trust Him anyway: *"Trust in God; trust also in Me"* (John 14:1 NIV). Would Jesus command you to do something that was impossible for you to do? Of course not. By renewing your mind and emotions through His Word, you can weed out the selfish thinking of this American culture; by walking in the Spirit and knowing the Word of God, you can put hurts, rejections, and disappointments behind you and overcome your fleshly nature; and by the power of God, you can defeat your lying enemy.

What Is Trust?

If you are to make any progress toward reclaiming trust in your life, we must all be working with the same definition of "trust." Words are critical to our thinking. Words define, characterize, and become a substitute for the idea or thing to which we apply them. *Words actually create the reality of what they symbolize for us.* In her autobiography, *The Story of My Life*, Helen Keller describes her experience as a blind and deaf child. With only her senses of taste, touch, and smell intact, she groped through her family's home like a wild animal. Unable to define her needs or what she desired to meet them, she flew into tantrums and rages in her frustration. Without a word attached to an idea or object, she could not effectively think about them, nor express her thoughts and needs—let alone higher concepts—to another person.

You may be able to visualize a cat and think about it without using words, but how do you visualize "freedom" or "democracy" or "trust"? We learn the majority of our words from our families and culture, but often these definitions may be distorted in some way, depending on the bias of our teachers. If your definition of trust is twisted, then we have just uncovered the first problem. For the purposes of this book, we have chosen the following definition from Webster's dictionary because it is widely accepted, clear, concise, and consistent with the way "trust" is used in the Bible. Webster's defines "trust" as:

> 1. firm belief or confidence in the honesty, integrity, reliability, justice, etc. of another person or thing; *faith*; reliance.
> 2. confident expectation, anticipation, or hope (to have trust in the future).[3] (Emphasis ours.)

Our first goal for you in learning to trust again is to develop a *firm belief and confidence in the honesty, integrity, reliability, and justice of God and His Son Jesus.* You must develop your faith in Him; you must learn that you can rely on Him; and you must develop a *confident anticipation* for the future plans He has for you.

To trust God is the same as having faith in Him. Remember what the Bible says about faith:

> *And without faith it is impossible to please God, because anyone who comes to Him must believe that He exists and that He rewards those who earnestly seek Him* (Hebrews 11:6 NIV).

So belief in God's existence and in the fact that He rewards diligent seekers is a necessary ingredient of genuine trust.

Our secondary goal is for you to learn to trust God as *He works through other people.* Though the Scriptures warn, *"Do not put your trust in princes, in mortal men, who cannot save"* (Ps. 146:3 NIV), you can trust in people as the life and attributes of Jesus are formed in them. The apostle Paul wrote to the Galatian church, *"My dear children, for whom I am again in the pains of childbirth until Christ is formed in you"* (Gal. 4:19 NIV). In other words, Paul recognized that even though these believers had gotten off base in their thinking, they still were in the process of maturing, just as children are in the process of becoming adults.

When the life of Jesus is manifested in a person's life, then you can place a degree of trust in that person. *You are really trusting God, who is at work in that person.*

We understand that accomplishing these goals is no easy task, but think of them as your down payment on the keys to that car. And remember: *With God, all things are possible.*

ENDNOTES

1. This metaphor was articulated by Derek Prince in *God Is a Matchmaker* (Grand Rapids, MI: Chosen Books, 1986).

2. An entire force of demonic powers from what Colossians 1:13 calls *"the domain* [or kingdom] *of darkness"* wars against the Kingdom of God. But we refer to these forces as a whole as simply "the liar," based on their satanic leader's main strategy.

3. *Webster's New World Dictionary, Third College Edition,* Victoria Neufeldt & David B. Guralnik (eds.) (New York: Simon & Schuster, Inc., 1988).

CHAPTER 6

Help, I Lost My Trust!

*"When a man has no reason to
trust himself, he trusts in luck."*

—Nineteenth-century American
journalist Ed Howe

*"Recognition is the beginning of recovery…whatever
you can tolerate you can't change."*

—Mike Murdock

❖·❖❖❖·❖

You Have to Trust in Something

People intrinsically want to trust in someone or something.
Trust is a building block of our personality. As babies we learn to
trust that our parents will come when we cry and will meet our
needs. As children we trust them to pick us up from school and

provide us with food and clothing. Our lives are built upon trusting that everyday events will happen as we expect.

We also learn to trust in people, some more than others. Most young children trust their parents implicitly. Every day, parents entrust their children to teachers and coaches. They also warn their kids not to trust strangers. By the time most children reach their teens, they have developed some sort of gauge to evaluate others and determine whether or not they can trust them. In the long run, everyone must trust someone or something, even if it is only himself.

Remember my (Ed's) tribulation with the broken leg? I had to trust in the judgment and ability of the physical therapist rather than my own flesh. My leg was screaming, "Stop, you're going to kill me!" But I knew that in order to regain its full use, I had to make my leg uncomfortable for a time. If I had listened to my leg, I would be disabled today. But because I listened to sound judgment and employed trust in someone who knew how to heal my leg better than my leg itself did, I am completely healed.

I could have responded to that trial with what I call a "turtle mentality." That is, when a person feels threatened, he withdraws, turtlelike, into his shell and refuses to come out. He begins to operate in isolation. The problem is that he can't eat, see, move around, or do anything until he comes out. He may feel safe inside his shell, but there is no room for relationships, no room for fun, no room for excitement, *no life!*

Mine was a choice between a physical disability and physical health. I certainly would not be able to ski today if I'd listened to my leg and not trusted the therapist. For me the choice was easy. I want you to acquire this type of perspective on the choice to trust or not to trust so that your decision will be easy also.

Regarding my leg, nobody was trying to persuade me to listen to my leg's opinion. My friends and family all knew what was right for me and held me accountable to endure the pain of physical therapy. However, when it comes to trusting God, the decision is not so easy because the liar is continually whispering his persuasions for us to make the wrong decision.

The Liar's Anti-Trust Strategy

The liar continually tries to conform you to the rebellious ways of his kingdom. He's really not very creative and uses the same methods over and over again. God's intention was that your intrinsic need to trust be fulfilled by Him, because He is the only one who is always trustworthy. God is the only one who will never violate your trust. However, the liar, who is not ignorant of your intrinsic need to trust, manipulates it against you. How does he do this? He does it by what I call the *Anti-Trust Strategy.*

The liar's strategy operates in two phases:

1. He gets you to trust in philosophies, things, or persons other than the true God.

2. When those fail you, he persuades you not to trust in anyone or anything. This promotes rebellion (against God) within your heart.

First he deceives you into trusting in things that will let you down—idols, other gods, false identities, counterfeits of the true living God[1]—that lead you away from trusting the true God. He knows that these things will never prove trustworthy. After they inevitably fail, the liar moves in with his lies, distortions, and misinterpretations, persuading you never to trust anyone or anything again. By not trusting in God, you enter into rebellion against His best plan for your life.

Bob has put Pastor Ted on a pedestal. He believes that Pastor Ted can do no wrong, that he always speaks the words of God, that he is the perfect Christian, abounding in wisdom and understanding. The liar has deceived Bob into making Pastor Ted—a mere man—into an idol. But when Pastor Ted makes a mistake in handling a situation, or says something that touches an exposed nerve in Bob's life, or even falls into sin, then what happens to Bob? He feels hurt, betrayed. The liar says, "Bob, these pastors are all alike.

You were stupid to trust him! If you're smart, you'll never trust another pastor again!" What do you think Bob will do?

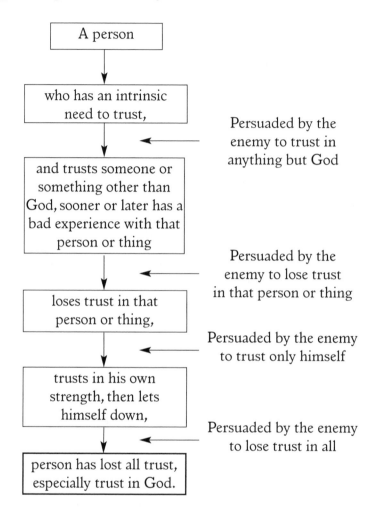

Why does the liar want to steal your ability to trust? He knows that if he can reduce your capacity to trust God, he is also removing your shield of faith. And the shield of faith extinguishes all the fiery darts of the enemy (see Eph. 6:16). So without the shield of faith, you are defenseless against his other attacks. You become isolated from God and from your network of support, and you don't have the ability to defend yourself. You become like an island, as Paul Simon wrote in a song from the 1960s, "I touch no one and no one touches me."[2] We become "devil bait." Does a lion charge into the middle of an antelope herd and attack the strongest one? No, he looks for one that is hurt or sick and is straggling behind the others. Don't let yourself become that isolated, hurt antelope and set yourself up for the lion's attack. Make the right decision concerning trust.

The Sea Anemone

The reason people will not trust again after being hurt is no mystery. Have you ever seen how a sea anemone reacts when it gets poked by a curious beachcomber? It immediately closes up, pulling its tender tentacles into itself for protection. It doesn't open up again until it has been undisturbed for a long time. Many people react just like that critter when their trust has been violated—they withdraw and won't "come out" to trust anyone else.

In *Following the Equator*, Mark Twain wrote, "We should be careful to get out of an experience only the wisdom that is in it—and stop there; lest we be like the cat that sits down on a hot stove-lid. She will never sit down on a hot stove-lid again—and that is well; but also she will never sit down on a cold one any more."[3] These types of self-protective strategies work against you when it comes to trusting God.

Trust in God is the difference between the cruising and the crawling Christian. The following paragraphs present an actual case study, told in the subject's own words, of a woman named Lisa[4] who lost her ability to trust and how deeply it affected her life:

> My childhood was not one of traumatic abuse. I always had enough to eat and wear. I was raised in a Christian home back in the "good ole days" where my mother stayed home to raise us and my father was the breadwinner. The whole family went to church three times a week. That's the scary thing. I had everything going for me.
>
> No one would guess from the type family in which I was raised that I could have gotten so screwed up.

The problem was that my emotional needs were not met. I was a very sensitive child. I needed acceptance and unconditional love. I needed to know that I was valued and important. But how does a small child tell you that her emotional needs are not being met? I didn't know what was wrong. I thought that I was at fault, that I was not doing something right, that one day I would figure out what it was that they wanted from me and then they would love me and I would finally be happy.

My father ruled supremely in our home and all of us kids stood in fear of him. He could correct us with a glance that would leave us trembling inside. One of his most often used phrases was, "Children are to be seen, not heard." That one sentence communicated myriad thoughts: It told me that my opinions didn't matter, that adults did not want to be bothered with me, that I was a nuisance to be tolerated until I grew up and could be of practical use to someone.

I remember overhearing a phone conversation that my mother was having with one of her friends who had recently found out she was pregnant. My mother was sympathizing with the friend and telling her that neither I nor my younger sister had been planned. I remember going into the bathroom and crying. The seed of rejection found fertile ground in my already wounded heart.

I was continually compared to my oldest brother, who was a prodigy. As my father told stories about him, he would say, "If he can do it, so can you!" I know now that he was trying to encourage me. What he was trying to say was that I was just as talented as my older brother. But that is not what I heard at the time.

I grew up being shown that women were less valuable than men. I was offended at how my father treated my mother. He would belittle and intimidate her. I remember one particular incident when he wanted her to sign some legal papers but he didn't want her to know what he was up to (he was a bit of a skunk!) When she asked what the papers were for, he flew into a rage, screaming, "Just sign the stupid papers! Can't you trust me?" The more I saw him manipulate her, the angrier I got. I was angry at him for treating her so badly, and I became angry at her because she let him get away with it. I was also angry at her for being emotionally needy—she was weak.

It didn't take long to get to the place where I didn't trust my father. I had seen him manipulate for his own selfish gain too many times. Based on his behavior, I began to make judgments about men: *"Men are selfish. Everything they do is strictly to promote their own gain. It does not matter how they try to disguise their motives, they are secretly working on their own agendas. You are just a pawn in the scheme of things, something to be conquered or used while they are on their way somewhere else."* Finally, after all the judgments were in, I made a vow. *"I'm not going to be emotionally vulnerable to my father or any other man."*

I became skeptical of any man who was nice to me. The first questions that would run through my mind were *"Why is he being nice to me? What does he want from me?"*

Naturally, my perspective of God was colored by my relationship with my father. I felt like God was waiting to catch me making a mistake so He could punish me. On one hand, I truly loved God, but on the other I was afraid of Him. I did not believe that He loved me for who I was, but rather He only loved me for what I could accomplish for Him or how well I obeyed His commands, just as I believed that my father loved me conditionally.

For fear of being treated the way I saw my mother being treated, I lumped all men in the same category as my father. I made God in the image of my father rather than the other way around. When I saw my father's weaknesses, instead of running to God, I ran away.

Because her father had manipulated and emotionally abused Lisa and her mother so many times, Lisa had vowed never to trust him. What would you have expected Lisa to do? To keep getting hurt by him repeatedly? She withdrew from him just like the sea anemone that retracts its tentacles from danger. Certainly he did not manipulate her all the time, but too often he did. How was she to know the difference? She vowed not to trust him just like the cat that won't ever jump on a stove lid, whether it's hot or cold. She became like a permanently closed sea anemone.

Surface Structures Versus Deep Structures

You may have heard the adage, "Beauty is only skin deep, but ugly goes to the bone." But I say, "Beauty is only skin deep, but love goes clear to the bone." This saying illustrates the ideas of *surface structures* and *deep structures*. By this we mean that there are two levels of reality—the behaviors that may be seen and the unseen motives behind those behaviors.[5] In Lisa's case, her lack of relationship with her father is a surface structure, while the loss of trust that caused it is a deep structure. The problem is not that Lisa doesn't trust her father—he's given her reason to do that; it is that she lost trust in *all men* due to her father's actions and now refuses to have meaningful relationships with any of them.

So loss of trust is a deep structure out of which develop the surface structures of the problems and hang-ups that torment people.

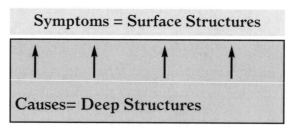

Symptoms = Surface Structures

Causes= Deep Structures

**We must cure the cause
not treat the symptoms.**

If you are a Christian, you must understand how trust or a lack of trust becomes a foundation for your motives and actions. You must also learn how to regain lost trust so you can have the abundant life that Jesus promised.

Faith in God Upholds Your Trust

The previously mentioned shield of faith that extinguishes the "flaming arrows of the evil one" is established upon your trust in God. When you think that God is not answering your prayers or that He failed to protect you in an adverse situation, the liar tempts you to make a judgment against God. If you lose sight of the fact that God knows what He is doing with your life and start to believe that He has forgotten you, you may bail out on God and choose not to trust Him anymore.

In these situations, your faith acts as a shield for your trust. In fact, you can *"know that in all things God works for the good of those who love Him, who have been called according to His purpose"* (Rom. 8:28 NIV).

You must say to yourself, "God has *not* let me down! I *choose* to wait upon Him until His faithfulness is manifested. God is *at work* in this painful situation and I will emerge from it a conqueror." However, this does not mean that every time you trust God He will give you what you want. That is an immature view of how God works. Like the wise and good Father that He is, He will give you what you need, which may look nothing like what you prayed or trusted Him for. You need to expand how you view "what God wants for you."

That attitude of stalwart trust is manifested in a determination to give thanks to God no matter how a situation is working out. The psalmist Asaph wrote, *"He who sacrifices thank offerings honors Me, and he prepares the way so that I may show him the salvation of God"* (Ps. 50:23 NIV).

You must also tell yourself—though it may be a sacrifice—"I will praise God for His faithfulness even though I cannot yet see the victory." This attitude of praise "prepares the way" for God to intervene on your behalf. As you then wait patiently, you will experience God's goodness in the midst of your circumstances.

Why Christians Must Trust God

Trust is absolutely essential to Christianity. Remember, trust is the key that starts the car. God has decreed that anyone who wants His blessings must trust in Him; otherwise that person will be cursed. This is the deal that God, in His wisdom, has offered us. If you have a problem with this, talk to God about it. He even put it in writing:

> This is what the Lord says: "Cursed is the one who trusts in man, who depends on flesh for his strength, and whose heart turns away from the Lord. He will be like a bush in the wastelands; he will not see prosperity when it comes. He will dwell in the parched places of the desert, in a salt land where no one lives. But blessed is the man who trusts in the Lord, whose confidence is in Him" (Jeremiah 17:5-7 NIV).

Additionally, the Book of Psalms opens with these words:

> Blessed is the man who does not walk in the counsel of the wicked or stand in the way of sinners or sit in the seat of mockers. But his delight is in the law of the Lord, and on His law he meditates day and night (Psalm 1:1-2 NIV).

This psalm goes on to compare this godly man to a tree growing beside a stream of water with strong roots bringing up nutrients from the soil, and leafy branches that never fail to bear fruit.

Webster's definition of trust contains the key words *faith* and *hope*. "Faith" is a synonym for trust. A person who says, "I don't trust you" is basically saying, "I don't have faith in you." So to lack trust in God is also to lack faith in God. The Bible says, *"Without faith it is impossible to please God"* (Heb. 11:6 NIV).

Jesus gave His followers a "word picture" in a well-known teaching called the Sermon on the Mount. His verbal illustration described two houses—one built high up on solid ground above the erosive force of the waves crashing on the shore, and the other built right on the beach. In the devastation that occurred in the coastal city of New Orleans during Hurricane Katrina in 2005, Americans saw vivid live images of the havoc wreaked upon buildings constructed on sand, while structures built on higher ground survived.

In Jesus' story, the houses themselves, apparently, were basically the same. The difference in their ability to withstand the forces of nature lay in their locations. Jesus classified the homebuilders as "wise" and "foolish"—wise to build on solid rock, foolish to build on shifting sand. He likened the wise builder to a person who hears His teachings and obeys, and the foolish builder to a person who hears His teachings but does not act upon His words—meaning, whether or not they trusted Him enough to do what He said.

The Christian who does not trust God is the man who builds his house upon the sand.

Because God is perfectly trustworthy, the worst insult you can pay to Him is not to trust Him. Our Christian walk is fundamentally a relationship with God made possible by our faith in His Son, Jesus. However, many people today profess faith in God but are not able to trust His guidance and leadership for their lives. The liar has deceived these people into becoming self-reliant—depending on themselves for answers in every situation.

The apostle Paul, who did not rely on himself but on God, exhorted believers to emulate his example. He wrote to the church at Corinth, saying, *"Indeed, in our hearts we felt the sentence of death. But this happened that we might **not rely on ourselves but on God**, who raises the dead"* (2 Cor. 1:9 NIV).

Toward the end of his life, Paul found himself imprisoned in a cold, damp cell, where he easily could have become depressed and lost his faith in God. He had begun his career as a reputable Pharisee, with the educational equivalent of a doctorate in religion, an expert regarding the Jewish customs and ceremonial laws. Paul could have gained fame and wealth among the religious leaders of his day. He was well on his way toward those goals when the Lord stopped him in his tracks, brought him to his knees, and presented him with a different—a Heavenly—agenda. This agenda rewarded his obedience to God with criticism, beatings, ostracism, imprisonment, and eventually, death.

How did Paul react to this turnabout in his fortunes? He wrote to his friends at Philippi, *"Whatever was to my profit I now consider loss for the sake of Christ. What is more, I consider everything a loss compared to the surpassing greatness of knowing Christ Jesus my Lord, for whose sake I have lost all things. I consider them rubbish, that I may gain Christ"* (Phil. 3:7-8 NIV).

If faith and trust are synonymous, how can you have faith in God unto salvation, yet not trust Him to move and work in your life? This is a serious problem calling into question the foundation of your Christianity—your faith.

I believe that most believers are neither totally self-reliant nor totally trusting in God. Only one person in all of history—Jesus—trusted God 100 percent of the time in every situation. The rest of us are somewhere in between self-reliance and God-reliance.

The great theologian, Dr. Francis Schaeffer, asked, "How should we then live?" The Bible responds, *"Trust in the Lord with all your heart and lean not on your own understanding"* (Prov. 3:5 NIV). Some people trust only in themselves. But themselves is all they have. As Christians, however, we have the option and the privilege of trusting in God. The *object* of our trust is crucial.

Let's get down to the issue: Is God reliable and trustworthy? Can He be trusted to act on behalf of your good in all areas of your life? What's your answer?

ENDNOTES

1. These are all what Jeremiah 2:13 calls *"broken cisterns that can hold no water."*

2. Paul Simon, "I Am a Rock," 1965.

3. Mark Twain, "Pudd'nhead Wilson's New Calendar," Following the Equator, http://mark-twain.classic-literature.co.uk/following-the-equator/ebook-page-45.asp.

4. Not her real name.

5. Jack L. Daniel & Geneva Smitherman, "How I Got Over: Communication Dynamics in the Black Community," in D. Carbaugh, ed., *Cultural Communication and Intercultural Contact* (Hillsdale NJ: Lawrence Erlbaum Associates, Publishers, 1990), 27.

CHAPTER 7

Judgments and Generalization and Vows, Oh My!

"Watch your thoughts; they become words. Watch your words; they become actions. Watch your actions; they become habits. Watch your habits; they become character. Watch your character; it becomes your destiny!"

—Frank Outlaw

Your self-reliant flesh sabotages trust. By this, I (Ed) mean that the process by which you make sense of your world and which controls your decision-making is easily influenced by the liar and can work powerfully against you. You must understand how your mind works if you want to understand the business of trust.

To function normally, people need a sense of order. Every week, Monday follows Sunday and is followed by Tuesday, Wednesday, and so on. Our calendars and clocks bring some sense of order to our schedules. We trust that flicking a little switch on a wall will fill a room with light, and that flicking it in the opposite direction will turn the lights off. If we cannot trust that certain events will happen predictably, then our lives will become chaotic.

Imagine what it would be like trying to drive if you could not trust what other drivers were going to do. What if you couldn't be sure that other vehicles would stay in the correct lane of traffic or that they wouldn't slam on the brakes in front of you without a reason? What if you could not depend on your own brakes to stop your car when you wanted? You'd probably conclude that it is safer to rely on another mode of transportation than to try to drive anywhere.

In similar fashion, you expect a certain consistency in your relationships with friends and relatives and other aspects of life. A recent movie, *In Her Shoes,* portrays the story of two sisters: Maggie and Rose. Rose, the stable, mature, older sister holds down a corporate job and lives a respectable, if boring, life. Her younger sister, Maggie, the perpetual party girl, is unreliable, impulsive, alcoholic, and a bit of a thief. Rose feels protective toward Maggie and bails her out of one mishap after another. Maggie moves into Rose's apartment and soon has her clothes and litter strewn from one room to another, all of which Rose tolerates. But after Rose catches Maggie in bed with her boyfriend, Rose finally says "enough," and kicks Maggie out of her apartment and out of her life.

The only thing consistent about Maggie is her unpredictability. If someone claiming to be a loyal friend or relative habitually misuses, manipulates, and treats you with disrespect, then—if you have healthy boundaries—you will probably avoid that person or cut off the relationship.

Judgments

Beginning in childhood, you've continually taken note of and judged other people's behavior. These judgments are formed in terms of how their actions affect you—whether their behavior brings you pain or pleasure physically or emotionally. You might think things like *That feels good; That hurts; I like that; I don't like this;*

He is mean; She is nice, and so on. As you've matured, you've learned how friends, relatives, and other acquaintances are supposed to treat one another. When someone does not treat you according to what you define as "normal," you determine that something is wrong, so in order to try to make yourself more comfortable, you may confront or avoid that person.

Such judgments can begin at an early age, even in infancy. Though not always consciously verbalized, these judgments may exist as feelings. They become imbedded in your memories. The episodes that you judge do not even have to happen to you. You may form judgments based on events you've witnessed in others' lives.

Taking Offense for Others

I can look through any daily newspaper and not read far before becoming angry. Our society is inundated with incidents of sense-less crimes. Recently, the 11-year-old son of members of a sister church died while in the care of a foster home. Amid a continuing police investigation, they are considering filing charges against employees of the foster care home for his wrongful death. The boy's Sunday school teacher, a friend of mine, was outraged at the death. He took offense for that boy who was unable to defend himself.

When we take offense for others, we make judgments that are just as strong as if we ourselves were the victims. Lisa (in Chapter 6) took offense for the way her father treated her mother. The judgments she made regarding that treatment affected her deeply.

Vows

As you form these judgments about your experiences and relationships, you begin to see certain patterns. At this point you can make a vow to guide you in your interactions with that person or experience. Webster defines a vow as: "a solemn promise or pledge, esp. one made to God or a god, *dedicating oneself to an act, service, or way of life.*" For example, when Mark Twain's cat jumped on the stove, it made the following judgments: "That's hot; that hurts; I don't like it." These judgments led to a vow: "I'm never going to jump on a stove again." This vow now protects her from getting burned in the future.

Vows vary in intensity from weak to powerful. A direct correlation exists between the power of the vow and three major contributing factors: Intensity, Frequency, and Currency. The strength of the vow determines how much it will influence our decisions and behavior. Here are three rules about vows:

1. The more traumatic an experience, the more powerful the resulting vow—*Intensity*.

2. The more often an experience, the more powerful the resulting vow—*Frequency*.

3. The more recent the experience, the more powerful the resulting vow—*Currency*.

What are the implications of these rules? If you suffered similar types of trauma more than once and not long ago, *you probably won't let yourself get into that situation again!*

Recalling Lisa's experience, she could never be sure if her father was behaving kindly out of genuine affection or for some manipulative scheme. She ultimately concluded that the risk of trusting him and being wrong outweighed the hoped-for benefits that never materialized. In evaluating her experiences with her father, Lisa made *judgments* about them—some good and some bad. Then, on the basis of whether these numerous judgments weighed for or against her father, Lisa formed a *vow* to guide her in future decisions in that relationship.

She vowed that she would never trust her father. Lisa did not realize that this entire process probably happened beyond the realm of her awareness; it is inherent in the human reasoning process. She probably never said aloud, "I will never trust my dad again," yet the unspoken vow held just as much, if not more, power over her as if she had spoken it. Often, a person makes judgments and forms vows without awareness of doing so.

Regarding the area of trust, I (Ed) have never counseled anyone who did not make one or more vows—consciously or subconsciously—to not ever trust again.

Don't misunderstand what I'm saying here. Vows are not all bad. Sometimes they are good—they can protect you from bad situations, and they can help you make self-protective decisions, especially when there is no time to adequately size up a situation. It is healthy to vow never to touch a hot stove, or to not trust a manipulative father. However, more often than not, you make vows that drastically affect your ability to have healthy relationships.

When it comes to relationships with others, your vows generally lead you to withdraw, or they're destructive to your ability to even form relationships. Vowing to not touch a hot stove will protect you; *a vow that you will never trust anybody again will devastate your life.*

Generalization

Complicating the issue of judgments and vows are the problems that arise from the next step in the reasoning process—*generalization.*

In an experiment designed to learn more about "conditioned emotional reactions," researchers John B. Watson and Rosalie Rayner presented a white laboratory rat before 11-month-old Albert.[1] When Albert reached toward the rat, the researchers scared the boy with a loud noise by striking a metal bar. After only two of these "tests," little Albert withdrew his hand when the rat nosed it.

A week later, the researchers presented the rat without the noise to see if Albert would still be afraid of the rat. He was; classical conditioning had occurred. At the mere presence of the rat, Albert would cry or crawl away. He had been jolted by that "scary" noise so consistently that he associated the fear it caused in him with the rat.

The following week, the researchers placed a white rabbit in front of Albert. The child cried and tried to crawl away. The boy had *generalized* his fear of the white rat to the white bunny and any other white furry object. He was even afraid of cotton balls, a fur coat, and a Santa Claus mask.

Notice that Albert was only *11 months* old when these experiments took place. The researchers never reconditioned him to no longer fear white furry objects or rats. Who knows? He may have required counseling later in life to undo the conditioning of that experiment. As an adult, he probably didn't remember the experiment; it didn't physically hurt him, and it was not particularly extensive. Yet, I conjecture that the negative effects of his experience may have reached into his adulthood.

Within this experiment are two significant points to keep in mind as we learn about trust:

1. Albert's fear remained even when its cause (the loud noise) was absent.

2. Albert generalized his fear to other similar, though unrelated, situations.

A baby's fear of loud noises is perfectly normal, but a fear of white furry objects is not. Generalization can be intensely powerful. Webster defines generalization as "to infer or derive a *general* law or precept from *particular* instances" (emphasis mine).

Albert may have evaluated the particular instance of the white rat experiment and made a generalization (or a vow) something like this: "I don't like this rat and I'm steering clear of it. Furthermore, I'm steering clear of anything that even reminds me of it." The real problem in such cases is not the vow itself, but the generalization of the vow to apply to other situations.

Generalization complicates a vow because you tend to apply the vow to an inappropriate situation—much as Albert did with his fear of furry white things. Remember Mark Twain's cat? She won't even jump on a cold stove now. Similarly, Lisa's problems stemmed not from her vow of mistrusting her father, but from her generalization of that vow to all men—*and to her image of God.*

"Impossible," you say. "That's not logical! How can fear of a white rat be translated into a fear of Santa Claus?" Yes, it is logical.[2] The logic is not found in the particular experiences but *is embedded in the reasoning process.* The particular experiences are the *surface structures.* The *deep structure* is the reasoning process at work in these situations.

Lisa's relationship with her father and the resulting vows and generalizations are not unique; counselors see similar patterns in their clients all the time. We trust that you recognize the danger of forming a general rule based on just one particular event or experience. The foolishness of forming a general rule about all relationships based on one bad relationship should also be evident.

Can you see where this process may have affected your life during hurtful situations? Perhaps you have seen the worst come out in Christians through a church split and have decided that deep down all Christians are hypocrites. Perhaps you are a pastor who let a new member serve in your church, and that person betrayed you. Now, because of your hurt, you allow no one to serve unless he or she has attended for at least a year. Maybe your father treated you as inconsiderately as Lisa's father treated her, and now you don't trust any man or even God inasmuch as He is called your Father.

Exactly How Does the Liar Get Into the Middle of All This?

Do not suppose for a minute that the liar does not understand the process of judgments, vows, and generalization. On the contrary, he is well acquainted with it and strategically uses it against us. In fact, his motto could be, "Kick 'em while they're down." Recall that the liar's Anti-Trust Strategy does two things: 1. It convinces us to trust in replacements for the true God and 2. it persuades us to not trust at all and to rebel against God.

The liar steps in and implements this strategy when you are least able to defend yourself. You might be too young or immature to fully understand what is going on, or you might be too emotionally involved to think clearly. The liar persuades you to not trust by convincing you to:

1. Make incorrect judgments.

2. Form trust-destroying vows.

3. Overgeneralize.

Incorrect Judgments

The liar will deceive you into making judgments based on error or inaccurate information. People form most of their judgments and vows by the time they are teenagers. Not until they are older, wiser, and more mature are adults able to judge experiences more objectively. Children and teens simply do not have enough knowledge to see "the big picture." Albert didn't know what was making the loud noise; he just knew it was sudden and unpleasant, it hurt his ears, and he associated it with the rat. Lisa didn't know what emotional abuse was or that it was wrong.

The Bible says, *"Train up a child in the way he should go, even when he is old he will not depart from it"* (Prov. 22:6). At every opportunity the liar sneaks in and performs as much of this training as he can. He knows that it is much easier to form the thought processes of a child than of an adult. That's why in many instances a person's emotions from a childhood trauma need to be healed before progress can be made toward wholeness. Changing the thinking patterns of an adult is difficult because of the accumulation of judgments and vows that are already in place. It is hard, but not impossible, to change all this. And you have taken the first step: You want help; you want to change. That's why you are reading this book.

Destructive Vows

Remember, the power of the vow stems from the *intensity, frequency,* and *currency* of the bad experience. Ultimately, the liar's goal is to get you to vow something like "I will never trust anyone or anything other than myself again!" It's worse when you do not even trust yourself. A man with difficulty trusting said, "I promised myself a year ago that I would never get into this business again [he was a salesman] and now, here I am. If I can't trust myself to keep a promise to myself, how can I ever trust anybody?" The liar had robbed him of all ability to trust.

The liar gets seriously involved in this process when it comes to your relationship with God. He will use every trick in the book (and even put words into your mind) to cause you to form error-filled judgments about God and encourage you to make vows destructive to a good working relationship with Him.

Keep in mind the liar's Anti-Trust Strategy: He will help you set up idols, let them fall, and then encourage you to make judgments and a vow that will destroy your ability to trust. The liar often says something like, "If God is 'all powerful,' then He could have prevented this bad thing from happening to you, but He didn't, did He? God must not love you, or this never would've happened." If you believe such lies, you might conclude, "God let me down. I'm never going to trust Him for anything again."

Many people decide that God *perpetrates* the *bad things* that happen. Friend, you don't see the big picture if you believe something like that. One of the liar's favorite tricks is to hit you over the head, hide the bat behind his back, and point his finger at God when you look to see who did it.

Forgive me for repeating, but I cannot overemphasize the importance of these two facts: 1. The shield of faith extinguishes the flaming arrows of the evil one. 2. This shield of faith is established upon your trust in God. Have faith that God loves you and has good plans for your life.

> *"For I know the plans I have for you," declares the Lord, "plans to prosper you and not to harm you, plans to give you hope and a future"* (Jeremiah 29:11 NIV).

Overgeneralization

When you place your trust in someone and he or she lets you down, the liar helps you to generalize that experience as much as possible. Remember that generalization means "to derive a *general law* from a *particular instance.*" Lisa generalized her distrust of her father to all men and to God. Had she married before learning how to trust again, she would never have been able to trust her husband.

Because generalizing is such a natural part of your reasoning process, it doesn't take much work on the liar's part to twist your thinking.

How the Liar Uses Others to Help Destroy Your Trust

Not only will the liar deceive you into thinking that God has injured you, but he will work through other people to add more injury, thereby further damaging your ability to trust. Often, when other people hurt you, the liar is the real culprit at work in them. Some people unknowingly hurt you by their insensitivity. When this happens, the liar takes advantage of the situation. He lies to you, saying that they hurt you on purpose. When you agree with that lie, you let error influence your judgment.

You cannot assume that you omnisciently know others' reasons for doing what they do. If you have been hurt and it seems remotely possible that the other person does not realize he has hurt you, go to him and talk about it. Wouldn't you want the opportunity to straighten things out if you had been the one who had unintentionally hurt the other person? What is the worst thing your friend could say? Something like: "Yeah, I did do that on purpose to hurt you!" That's what you would have figured anyway.

In fact, Jesus addressed this very type of relational glitch during His famous Sermon on the Mount. He said (and I'm paraphrasing), "You might be in the middle of writing out a check for a huge donation to your church. And then you suddenly remember the hurt look on your best friend's face when you made a joke at her expense. Well, put down your pen; forget about the donation for now. I'm more interested in you and your friend being reconciled than I am in your money. Once you're reconciled and your heart is right and pure, I will gladly receive your gift" (see Matt. 5:23-24).

So you might as well run the risk of rejection (which probably won't happen) and take the necessary steps to clear the air.

The Bullfight: Sometimes We Are the Real Problem

Some people *will* hurt you intentionally. Their reasons—be they greed, lust, selfish ambition, and so forth—always have their roots in the liar's work in that person's life. Look at this type of situation as a bullfight. You are the bull, the liar is the matador, and the person who hurt you is the red cape. Don't be the angry bull that always tries to get the cape while the matador dances away. Your real foe is the matador, whose goal is to kill you. On one of your furious charges, the matador will drive his sword down into your back, piercing your heart, and killing your ability to trust (or do anything else for that matter) ever again.

Like the matador's red cape, the person who hurts you is merely carrying out the desire of your foe, the liar. Look at the big picture. Do not misidentify your enemy in these matters. Your life depends on identifying him correctly as the liar.

Summary

Here is a list of what you've learned so far:

1. Individuals make judgments about their or others' experiences. These judgments may be correct or incorrect.

2. As a pattern of judgments develops, individuals make vows to guide their future decisions.

3. Individuals generalize their experiences from familiar situations to unfamiliar ones.

4. Individuals often inappropriately generalize their experiences. This is called overgeneralization.

5. The liar encourages overgeneralization in a way that will confuse or hurt you. He also encourages incorrect judgments in critical areas of your life. His goal is to get you to make vows that are destructive to your ability to trust.

6. The liar will use other persons in any way he can to shatter your trust. Sometimes that other person knows it and sometimes he doesn't.

These are important principles for you to understand. Blaming everything on the liar and praying for deliverance is not going to solve the problem. You must undo the deception that he has helped put in your mind. Understanding how your mind works is critical to this process.

ENDNOTES

1. J.B. Watson & R. Rayner, "Conditioned Emotional Reactions," *Journal of Experimental Psychology*, 3(1), (1920), 1-14.

2. Inductive reasoning is a well-understood form of logic where conclusions are reached by moving from the specific to the general.

CHAPTER 8

Breaking the Trust Barrier

"Problems aren't meant to break us;
problems are meant to make us."

—Dr. Frank Freed

We've established that three antagonistic forces—the world, the flesh, and the devil (whom we call the liar)—work against your ability to trust. Now you need to believe that it is possible to overcome these forces and reclaim your trust.

Some people believe that they've been hurt too badly to ever trust again: women like Mandy and Lisa whose trust has been violated by a selfish father or husband; grown-up baby Alberts who, as children, were used as someone's "experiment" in teaching or parenting. They may be churchgoers who've been let down or manipulated by a pastor. Such situations are, unfortunately, common.

But what about someone whose trauma has been even more extreme, such as sexual or ritualistic abuse? That person's trust has been not merely violated, but shredded. Even so, the process of losing trust follows the same sequence of judgments, resulting vows, and generalizations, only with multiplied intensity. Usually the lingering effects of the judgments, vows, and generalizations are too powerful for the victim to overcome by himself. Often, the liar has managed to attain complete domination of the wounded person's life. Yet a minister or layperson trained in applying biblical truth to life situations may be equipped to come alongside that person and help him break the domination.

Regaining Trust

Similar to losing trust, regaining trust requires a process. First, the spiritual and natural issues involved must be addressed. Second, any pride and pretensions that have resulted in self-reliance must be confessed and submitted to the sovereignty of Christ. In other words, Jesus must be seated on the throne of the wounded person's life. Third, the tangle of error-filled judgments and destructive vows that opened the door for this pretentious thinking must be unraveled.

If you are such a person, is your situation hopeless? No! If you have Jesus, you have the key already in your possession. Take it out and put it in the ignition. Just don't expect to leave your driveway and arrive at your destination instantly. Learning to trust again— like any learning experience—is a process.

A person who has lost his trust is like a burn victim in many respects. Here is an example. At the age of four, Sandra Tarlen was playing outside with her two brothers and several children who lived next door, while Sandra's father was burning leaves. One of the little boys threw a coffee can filled with gasoline into the fire. Flames exploded into little Sandra's face causing first-, second-, and third-degree burns. Yet the pain of her extensive injuries was slight compared to the treatment that followed. Doctors had to peel away layer after layer of charred and dead skin to allow them to reach healthy tissue under-neath. Each change of her bandages resulted in more physical agony.

As she grew older, her scar tissue—which would not stretch to accommodate her physical growth—became more pronounced and disfiguring, eventually requiring 22 reconstructive surgeries and skin grafts. Regular makeup wouldn't cover the scars and, without pores or "peach fuzz" to cling to, it would slide off in ex-treme heat. So Sandra couldn't even cover up her scars until years later when she found a makeup specially formulated to cover scars, birthmarks, and other skin imperfections.

Sandra's emotional scars were even more pronounced than her physical ones. Rejected by her father, an alcoholic, sexually abused by a neighbor, and gang-raped at age 13, Sandra turned to physical relationships for acceptance and affirmation. She had two children by age 17, and had been married four times before she turned 25. Her bitterness and anger brought on migraine headaches, ulcers, eating disorders, alcohol and drug abuse, even suicide attempts. However, her life turned around when she opened her heart to re-ceive God's love and forgiveness expressed through Jesus' death on the Cross on her behalf.

Like Sandra Tarlen's burns, broken trust takes time to heal. You must not expect that established patterns of thought and behavior will miraculously melt away, and you'll be able to trust God and others merely because you've decided that it would be good for you. Regaining trust is a multi-step process of *remembering, releasing, re-thinking, relearning,* and *reestablishing.*

Remembering

Just before the nation of Israel entered the Promised Land, Is-rael's great leader, Moses, made a final speech to them. Standing on the eastern side of the Jordan River, Moses—the man who had led the Israelites out of slavery in Egypt, through 40 years of wandering in the wilderness—reiterated the commandments and ceremonial laws that the Lord had revealed to him on Mount Sinai.

He said (and I paraphrase), "Listen up, Israel! And do everything I'm telling you today because it comes straight from the Lord's mouth—and He is the one and only true God. So don't you dare go worshiping idols. The God of the universe picked you out to be His people, and He wants you to obey Him. More than that, He wants you to love Him wholly, completely, and enthusiastically—and not just one day a week at a worship service. He wants you to *love* Him *all* the time and *think* about Him *all* the time and *talk* about Him *all* the time, so your kids will grow up knowing how great He is.

"In fact, to help you remember, He wants you to write down these words I'm telling you and tie them to your hands so that you'll see Him in everything you do. And He wants you to tie these words to your foreheads, so that you'll remember Him in all your thoughts. And, furthermore, He wants you to write them on the door frames of your houses, so that every time you go out of your house or come back inside, you'll remember Him."

What did they need to remember? Here's a brief list:

1. He is the one true God.

2. He loves them.

3. He wants them to love Him in return.

4. He delivered them from 400 years of slavery and set them free.

5. He destroyed a powerful army that was chasing after them.

6. He parted the Red Sea so they could walk over from Egypt, the land of their enslavement, to the Promised Land side.

7. He provided them with food and water for their 40-year journey through the desert.

8. He didn't allow their clothes to wear out.

9. He gave them laws to live by that set them apart from all the other nations in the world as His holy people.

Sounds easy enough, doesn't it? How could a person *not* love someone who has done so much for him? Yet, looking not far ahead into the future, God continued, "Now remember: You're going to get into this rich land and conquer the people living there so that you can live in their houses and harvest the crops that they planted. You're going to become overnight successes—you'll all be instantly wealthy and prosperous. Just, when that all happens, don't forget about the God who got you there" (see Deut. 6:6-12).

It's easy to be critical of the Israelites who so quickly justified Moses' warning and forgot God as they fell into disobedience and idolatry in the Promised Land. You and I probably never would have forgotten all that the Lord did for us, would we? Just like we wouldn't have bitten into the forbidden fruit like Adam and Eve did, right?

Of course, I'm being facetious. We repeat these types of sins every day—only not with such disastrous results.

So what does the Lord want *us* to remember?

1. He is the one true God.

2. He loves us.

3. He wants us to love Him in return.

4. He delivered us from a lifetime of slavery to sin and set us free.

5. He will destroy the powerful enemy that keeps chasing after us.

6. He parts the "red tape" of spiritual legalism so that we can walk in freedom and according to His promises.

7. He provides us with spiritual nourishment during our journey through this life.

8. He doesn't allow our spiritual covering to wear out.

9. He gives us His perfect law of love to live by that sets us apart as His holy people.

As we remember these truths, God gives us a "vision of trust." In other words, He reminds us of His goodness, wisdom and love and promises to work all things together for the good of those who love Him and are called to be His people and to be used for His purposes (see Rom. 8:28). When I (Pauly) find myself worrying about finances or relationships or work-related issues and so on, I get on my knees by the side of my bed and start to remember. I remember how miserable I was before I knew the Lord. I remember my confusion and insecurity and frantic search for acceptance. And then I remember how overwhelmingly grateful and peaceful I felt when I understood that my Messiah, Jesus, died for me and that God had forgiven me for all my self-induced misery. And as I remember these things, God brings me to that place of peace and gratitude once more.

Notice that the change in my attitude has nothing to do with a change in circumstances. Don't be mistaken—our vision of trust is not wishful thinking or a New Age-type of visualization of our desired outcome. The vision we need is based on the simple, unchanging Truth of who our God is. This vision has been compared to a solid rock, a firm foundation, an anchor for the soul, a light in the darkness.

After being arrested in Jerusalem for disrupting the peace merely by his controversial presence, the apostle Paul was onboard a ship bound for Rome in order to be tried before Caesar. A storm that raged for two weeks finally shipwrecked him, and all other 275 people aboard, on the island of Malta. Throughout the ordeal, Paul continually exhorted and encouraged the soldiers guarding him, telling them that they would all survive. How could he be so sure of that outcome? He'd known that he was going to have to suffer for the Lord's sake from the outset of his walk of faith, and he knew that before the end of his life he would stand trial before Caesar (see Acts 9:16; 21:10-15). So how could he die in a shipwreck? Paul had a vision of trust in where the Lord was taking him.

Furthermore, as he threw some wood that he'd gathered onto the fire, a viper clamped its deadly fangs onto his hand. What did Paul do? He shook the snake off into the fire and went about his business while the amazed natives looked on, expecting him to swell up or keel over at any moment.

Likewise, as you go about your daily business, a person or situation may "bite" or "latch on" to you. Just as Paul shook off the viper that bit him, so can you shake off the temptation not to trust again when it "bites" you. The puncture wounds hurt, but it's the venom that kills. The sting and pain of being let down or harmed will always hurt, but you don't have to let it poison and kill you. The venom—the choice not to trust—is what kills. God will protect you from the venom just as He did Paul if you maintain a vision of trust.

Acquire a vision of trust so that you can shake off the viper whenever you get bit.

Releasing

Mandy's mantra, *No man can be trusted,* became one of those songs she just couldn't get out of her head. But ultimately, she had to give up this preconception and judgment of all men, the lie that was based on her experience. She had to put the lie to death and give God the opportunity to show her His trustworthiness. In other words, she needed to *release* her situation into God's hands.

God commands us to forgive one another even as He has forgiven us. Often, out of obedience to Him, we choose, by faith, to forgive someone who has hurt us. But trust is a different matter. You may trust something (or someone) that isn't trustworthy, and you will suffer the consequences. You'll end up like the little pig who built his house with straw. One huff and puff from the big bad wolf, and that pig was seeking shelter elsewhere.

On an emotional and intellectual level, trust is earned through behaviors that merit trust. For example, if you step on my foot while shaking my hand, I'll dismiss it as an accident. If the next time we shake hands, you step on my foot again, I may think you're getting awfully clumsy. However, by the time you've stepped on my foot three times in a row, I'll be sure to stand back as I extend my hand. That is, I'll start to build a boundary to protect myself.

Such protection is healthy and natural. Yet, in certain abusive situations, a victimized person may lose the ability to assess his or her own level of pain and will be unable to say no to perpetrators of pain. Another may think that to be a "good" Christian, no matter how others misuse him (physical abuse, embezzling funds, manipulation, etc.), he's obligated to trust them. Such victimized individuals confuse forgiveness with overlooking harmful, destructive behaviors.

Trust is earned through consistent right behavior over time. Even then you need to trust God above all else, because any person, even a normally caring person, at any given time may violate your trust. You have no guarantees regarding another person's behavior.

The movie *The End of the Spear* tells the story of Mincayani, a Waodani tribesman in Ecuador, who, in 1956, participated in slaughtering five missionaries. Mincayani personally speared Nate Saint, whose four-year-old son, Steve, later went with his mother and the other widows to share God's love with the Waodani. Because of these women's determination to continue the work begun by their husbands, Mincayani and his tribe were redeemed and transformed from violent to peace-loving people. In the 1990s, Steve Saint and his family returned to Ecuador to work among the Waodani, and they lived with Mincayani's family. How could Steve trust the man who murdered his father? Only by the supernatural working of God in his heart.

Remember, your trust is not in man, but in God.

Rethinking

Such trust in God requires that you confront the lies in your life and, like Sandra Tarlen's doctors, peel away the dead layers of lies that coat your soul. This is a painful process of giving up the "old you," the person you've imagined yourself to be as you've paid attention to the liar's hogwash.

You must realize that you haven't lost your ability to trust; you've just placed your trust in untrustworthy things. Because those "things" (idols) have consistently failed, you have chosen not to trust in anything. You've become afraid to trust anything that even resembles those idols, but *you never lose your ability to trust.*

You trust your eyes and ears to give you correct perceptions; you trust the food you eat to nourish your body; you trust little switches on the wall to turn on your lights; you trust other drivers not to run you off the road. Every day you make decisions requiring you to trust in things beyond your immediate control. Trust is necessary for life.

Trust is also necessary for eternal life in God's Kingdom. Yet, ironically, when things don't go our way, our primary choice is often to not trust God and other people. The Bible tells us not to put our total trust in other people, but it *commands* us to trust in God. Trusting Him is not an option!

Trusting in God is a conscious choice. It requires us to rethink our options. Before I knew the Lord, I (Pauly) used to think that I needed to verbalize every thought that popped into my head. I thought this was being honest. But when the Lord entered my life, He started to make me uncomfortable with this impulsive blurting. Rather than being honest (which I considered a virtue), I began to hear the Lord suggest that I was being rude (not a virtue). I began to realize that there existed a space of time following the moment a thought entered my mind during which I could consider the relative merits of speaking it or keeping my mouth shut or at least tempering my language. Aha! Self-control! A fruit of the Spirit surfaced in my life. I now had the opportunity to trust God's leading and *adjust my thinking* about *what* I said and about *how* I said what I said.

Moreover, Scripture makes it clear that we are not the victims of our mind's random thoughts. The apostle Paul tells us to set our minds on things above (see Col. 3:2). And Paul told his friends at Philippi to think about specific things: whatever is true, noble, right, pure, lovely, admirable, excellent, or praiseworthy (see Phil. 4:8). So there's no need to obsess about worrisome things or fret about not being able to get a song or a thought out of your head. *If God's Word says that you can choose to focus on other specific things, then you must be able to do it.* When you're listening to a CD or MP3 and grow tired of a certain song, all you have to do is switch tracks. You can do the same thing with the "tapes" you play in your mind. You begin by making a conscious choice to "switch tracks" from selfish fleshly thoughts to godly ones.

At first, making these types of mental adjustments and choices is difficult. Then, as your habit patterns change and you experience the blessings of God because of your trust in Him, your progress becomes more rapid. To make this choice easier you must get to know God in a more profound way and on His terms, not yours.

Relearning

Several years ago, Alan and I went skiing with a group of friends. Non-skier that I am, I borrowed equipment from a friend. We got to the ski lodge, and I wrestled my feet into the boots, in a Cinderella's-stepsister sort of way. Then I locked those boots into metal bindings on the skis. Suddenly my feet were seven feet long!

After snowplowing wide S-shapes back and forth across the bunny hill, I decided I was ready to tackle a real run with Alan. I was just getting used to my awkward fiberglass-and-metal appendages, when the ski run curved—but I didn't. I slid right off the course and, taking advantage of my lack of expertise, a 12-foot-deep pile of snow jumped up and grabbed me, and I landed in it backside-first. I wasn't hurt; in fact it felt good to be lying there and resting for a bit. I looked down toward my feet, and those long, blue skis formed a perfect "X" with the tops pointing at the sky.

A few moments later, Alan came shushing up like Dudley Do-Right on skis and offered his advice. "You might want to bring your legs together and plant your poles on one side to push yourself back up again." Or some such nonsense.

"I don't even know which muscle to move to try to get my legs to come together," I responded.

"Well, if you don't want my help, then forget it," he replied and skied off down the hill, leaving me to my own devices. So much for Dudley Do-Right. I ended up taking off my skis and struggling to my knees and eventually to my feet and then back into my skis.

You see, even after Alan told me *what* to do, I still didn't know *how* to do it. And that, I believe, is also a problem for those of us who wrestle with this issue of trust. You know you're supposed to trust the Lord, and you want to trust the Lord. But you just don't know how to do it.

It's not that difficult, but it does require you to make some difficult choices. What makes these choices so difficult? One, they go against the grain of your feelings; and two, they require you to give up control to an outside party, namely God.

Here are the choices you need to make:

1. ***Believe that you can reclaim your trust.*** Do you believe this, or do you believe that you have been hurt so often and so deeply that you will never be able to trust again? The liar will tell you that you've been hurt too often to try again. God tells us that we can forgive—He will even help you to forgive—and that it's not too late to trust again. To whose voice will you listen? Whose message will you believe?

   The Bible teaches that trust is a *gift* from God. It says that He's given you everything you need for life and godliness through Jesus (see 2 Pet. 1:3 NIV). Trust is a necessary ingredient in God's "recipe" for life and godliness. His divine power, the Holy Spirit, gives you that trust.

   The Spirit also gives you the *ability* to trust God. He will give you, just as He gave Paul, the trust and confidence that God is at work in your life (see 2 Cor. 3:4). Paul said that love *"always trusts, always hopes, always perseveres"* (1 Cor.

13:7 NIV). The Holy Spirit gives you this godly type of love as you learn to live moment by moment in Jesus.

2. ***Trust wisely.*** You always have a choice about whom you are going to trust. So, trust in God, who never fails, not in earthly people or things, which have let you down in the past. And remember that the liar will continually hound you to choose anything other than the Lord and His Truth. Turn a deaf ear to his lies, and choose Truth.

3. ***Live in truth and the power of the Spirit.*** Your level of trust is directly related to how well you know God and His Word. To trust God you must know Him; and if you truly know Him, you *will* trust Him. You'll trust Him because He is *totally trustworthy.*

In order to accomplish change in your life, you need to retrain your mind to think according to God's patterns. You must know and believe what His Word says about Him. You already believe that if you confess Jesus as your Lord and have entered the Kingdom of God. Do not hurt yourself by ignoring those portions of His Word that expose your wrong beliefs and faulty thinking. Our minds are to be renewed by believing God's Word.

Your level of trust in God depends on how well you know God. As you know Him better, you will be able to trust Him more. The young Hebrew shepherd David was not afraid to fight the giant mercenary Goliath because David trusted God; and he trusted God because he knew God.

God has called you, like David, to know Him intimately by your understanding, experience, and prayer. You should know His qualifications and His attributes. And as you know Him more, you'll be able to:

...trust *Him* (see Ps. 71:1).

...trust *His Word* (see Ps. 119:42).

...trust *His name* (see Isa. 50:10).

...trust *His mercy* (see Ps. 52:8).

...trust *His Son, Jesus* (see Phil. 2:19).

You can know God by reading His autobiography, the Bible. It recounts the things He's done in the past, what He is doing now, and what He plans to do in the future. It expresses what God loves, what He hates, and what His deepest desires for His children are.

How often do you read God's Word? Getting to know God personally won't happen at a seminar, and it's highly unlikely that you'll be caught up into the third heaven as Paul was. Get to know God firsthand by knowing His Word; then perhaps He may give you some additional insights and personal applications.

On some occasions, people hear God speak to them through strong impressions, visions, dreams—rarely by an audible voice. Yet often that's the way people expect to be guided by Him. However, that is not the way God most often "speaks" to His people. The writer of the letter to the Hebrews writes, *"In the past God spoke to our forefathers through the prophets at many times and in various ways, but in these last days He has spoken to us by His Son"* (Heb. 1:1-2 NIV).

We can know God by knowing what His Son, Jesus, has spoken to us. The publishers of many versions of the New Testament put Jesus' words in red so that we may easily discern what He said. If you want to know God, know what Jesus taught.

You can know God by spending time with Him. You can include Him in your daily activities by beginning your day with prayer, asking for His support and help as you face the world. He has already promised that He will be with you always; so recognize His presence everywhere and in every situation (see Matt. 28:20). You do not have to face life alone. God is with you, so who can be against you? As you experience more of His faithfulness, you'll see more of His trustworthiness.

During my mid-20s, I (Ed) went through the heart-breaking experience of a divorce. This experience totally shattered my trust in women, relationships, and life in general. Many people in this situation, because of the hurt, will begin to "medicate" on unforgiveness, bitterness, alcohol, sexual addiction, overeating, other quick-fix relationships, busyness, or isolation.

God led me during this time to His Word. I began to "medicate" on His Word. I would spend hours each night reading and meditating upon the Word. There were times when I would read through a book of the Bible and have most of it memorized in one sitting. It was an awesome season of healing. As I read the Word, it became a "healing to my bones" (see Prov. 3:8). My trust began to return and be strengthened. What I had to learn and to trust in was this: If God is for me, who can be against me? As I started to trust God, I began a closer relationship with Him through prayer.

How much do you pray each day? Do you spend time getting to know God in prayer? Do you tell Him about your problems? Do you pour out your heart to Him and lean on Him, letting Him silently comfort you? Do you listen for His voice? Do you listen for His advice when you need it? Will you admit to Him that you don't know everything—He already knows that, anyway—and that you would appreciate hearing what He has to say?

We must know God on His terms, not on our own. Often we ask God for things out of immaturity or selfishness, and when we don't receive these things, we make judgments against God: "I don't understand why God doesn't answer my prayers; God must not like me!" When we're impatient for an answer, many of us conclude that God doesn't hear or care about our prayers. In reality, the answer may be on its way, and we bail out on God before it arrives.

Perhaps God withheld what you requested because He knew that it would ultimately cause you grief. Had you known God and sought Him in prayer you would have understood these things.

The liar is always right there to persuade you to see things on your own terms rather than God's. He will attempt to convince you that God is not trustworthy. He will assist you in making judgments and vows against God.

Does God indeed violate our trust or does He override our expectations of what *we think* should be the foundations of our relationship with Him? The Bible clearly defines the parameters of our relationship with God. We must not let our culture dictate those parameters. The world says relationships should be "give and take" or "50-50" or "You scratch my back and I'll scratch yours." The Word of God says that our relationship with Him is founded upon grace. He is not obligated to give us that grace but He does because He loves us.

God will never violate your trust. If you believe that He has violated your trust, then you need to quit pointing your accusing finger at Him, look in the mirror, and do some serious self-examination. In fact, true maturity is demonstrated by the apostle Paul who wrote from prison to his friends at Philippi, *"I consider everything a loss compared to the surpassing greatness of **knowing Christ Jesus my Lord,** for whose sake I have lost all things. I consider them rubbish, that I may gain Christ"* (Phil. 3:8 NIV).

People don't know God because they're too busy with themselves or preoccupied with other things. They're trying to find significance and meaning in life outside of knowing God.

In order to trust God, you must know God! You must know God according to the New Covenant revealed by His Word and not by the "patterns of the world." In other words, you need to unlearn worldly ways of thinking in order to relearn how to think and how to live God's way as described in His Word. Otherwise you will misunderstand the things God does or does not do in your life, resulting in error-prone judgments about Him. Such judgments on your part will lead to the types of vows that destroy your relationship with God.

Reestablishing

If you want to trust the Lord, know His Word! Your trust level may be low because you don't spend even one minute per day in the Word. You cannot trust God if you do not intimately know Him; and you cannot know Him except by His Word. And if you want to know His Word, you must set out with some discipline and intentionality to read and study the Bible.

How much time each week do you spend getting to know God? A person can earn a bachelor's degree from a university with about 2,000 hours of classroom study and 2,000 hours of homework. This is the minimum qualification needed to hold most professional positions in our culture. If the only study of God's Word you receive is a 60-minute sermon, three times per week, it would take you 25 years to know God as well as you know your occupation!

Read what His Word says, and take it at face value. Even as we speak today with synonyms and metaphors and hyperbole—"I'm so hungry I could eat a horse," "I almost died laughing," "That guy's a real turkey"—people in Jesus' day did, too. So when Jesus said, *"Take My yoke upon you and learn from Me…and you will find rest for your souls"* (Matt. 11:29), His audience knew that He didn't mean for people to put an actual wooden yoke on their shoulders. But they did understand that He meant to draw a comparison. Just as an ox wears a yoke so that its master can guide it when it's going to pull a plow, so we need to allow ourselves to serve and be guided by our Master, Jesus. And the end result of doing so will be rest for our souls.

By reading the Word and thinking about what it means and how it applies to you, you can learn what God desires for your life and have a "conversation" with Him. Learn about God's nature, His attributes, His ways, His thoughts, His power, His compassion, His wisdom, and His great love for you.

The following chapter will help you learn what God's Word says about trusting Him, but it is only a beginning point. Do whatever you need to do to develop a lifestyle of searching, studying, and reading your Bible. Sacrifice some of the mediocre TV shows you watch to spend time in God's Word daily. Do whatever it takes; it is worth any sacrifice to know God.

Trust God in your daily choices. After following all the suggestions we've listed, there still comes a time when you just have to step out and trust God. You probably already know that trust comes easily for you in some areas while others are more difficult. You need to begin working on the areas where you have trouble trusting Him. For some people, trust can be like skydiving or bungee jumping for the first time. Fear can hold you frozen at the point of commitment, just before you step into mid-air.

Take that first step into truly trusting God in your daily choices. Start with small things if you need to; God will meet you at your point of faith. If it's too easy, then it doesn't require faith. There must be a level of risk on your part.

Do you remember Lisa from Chapter 6? As she was praying about entering into the relationship that would later become her marriage, God spoke one word to her: *Risk!* She trusted God and today is happily married and has an exciting future ahead of her.

If you've been hurt in a relationship, try dating again. If you've lost your shirt in business, try a new venture. If friends have used you, try making a new friend. If you've been hurt by a white (brown, black, yellow, or purple-polka-dotted) person, try trusting again.

We call this "fighting with the opposite spirit," that is, overcoming evil with good. Don't let one person or situation from your past rule your entire life. I believe that there are three basic emotions: *fear,* which is "moving away"; *anger,* which is "moving against"; and *love,* which is "moving toward." My advice is to choose—and it is your choice—love. Fight with the opposite spirit and move toward; become a bridge builder, not a bridge burner.

You may believe that your situation was too devastating to ever try trusting again. This is exactly what the liar wants you to believe. The Hellers and I have counseled hundreds of people and heard every scenario over the years and we have never found a situation that God couldn't handle. However, whether people will allow God to handle it or not is a different story.

God is able to make all grace abound to you (see 2 Cor. 9:8). Some of us need more grace than others, but God has plenty to meet any need you have. Trust will become easier as you practice. I promise,

God will not disappoint or hurt you. Although knowing God makes the decision easier, there is nothing more I can say than, "Just do it."

Once you begin to develop a level of trust again, *hold onto it!* The liar will surely come and try to steal it away. If you think God let you down, go back to His Word and see what it says about your situation. Ask your pastor to help you sort through the confusing issues. Don't listen to the liar's untruths and half-truths and twisted truths and outright lies. Ask the Holy Spirit for discernment in sorting out the truth of a matter and discard any lies. When others disappoint you, shake off the "viper" and go on about your business.

Here is a brief summary of this chapter. You must regain your trust by following these five steps:

1. Remember.
2. Release.
3. Rethink.
4. Relearn.
5. Reestablish.

These days, you can find Sandra Tarlen counseling other women about how to gain victory over pain and bitterness and their own particular brands of scars. She speaks to audiences at churches and conferences about the healing power of forgiveness. And most importantly, she has allowed the dead layers of her self-reliance to be stripped away, down to the "healthy tissue" of new life in Christ. Her favorite Scripture verse says, *"If anyone is in Christ, he* [or she] *is a new creation; the old has gone, the new has come!"* (2 Cor. 5:17 NIV).

CHAPTER 9

I'm Not Moved by What I Feel; I'm Only Moved by the Word That's Real

*"I will, by my life's choices, prove
that the Word of God is true."*

—Ed Delph

———

In learning how to trust God again, many Christians run up against the same hurdle: They've become what I (Ed) call "Word-hardened." God describes this phenomenon through His prophet, Isaiah, in an often-misunderstood passage of Scripture:

Who is it He is trying to teach? To whom is He explaining His message? To children weaned from their milk, to those just taken from the breast?...To whom He said, "This is the resting place, let the weary rest"; and, "This is the place of repose"— but they would not listen. So then, the word of the Lord to them will become: Do and do, do and do, rule on rule, rule on rule; a little here, a little there—so that they will go and fall backward, be injured and snared and captured (Isaiah 28:9,12-13 NIV).

The publishers of the New International Version of the Bible give us insight into what's meant by "Do and do...rule on rule...a little here, a little there." A footnote tells us that the Hebrew for this phrase is *"sav lasav sav lasav kav lakav kav lakav."* And that it is possibly meaningless sounds or a mimicking of the prophet's words.

God is saying that Israel has heard the Word of the Lord so often that it has lost its meaning for them (like TV comedian Jerry Seinfeld's saying, "Yada, yada, yada") and that their injury and capture will soon follow. This passage holds a warning for us today: Listen to God. Do not let His words become meaningless sounds to you. Listen to God and let His Word permeate your spirit and change your life.

Coupled with a lack of knowledge of God, any vows you hold against Him render trusting impossible. The power of your judgments and vows to mold and conform your value systems and decision-making processes cannot be overstated. When an individual has a value system filled with error-prone judgments, that person is not able to make wise decisions. It's like having broken and worn-out tools for an important job. A seamstress needs to have sharp scissors to cut through fabric without shredding it. If her children (or husband) use those scissors to cut paper or string or packing tape—you get the idea—those scissors will become dull. Then when she needs them to cut out a pattern, they're nearly useless to her, especially for a fine fabric, like silk or satin.

OK, so maybe you men out there can't relate to sewing scissors. How about shaving with a dull razor blade? Or performing surgery with a dull scalpel? The point is that we all need high-quality tools for the high-quality tasks in life. Likewise, we need high-quality (or sound) judgment to make high-quality, sound decisions.

Because He knew God's Word, Jesus knew who He was, where He had come from and where He was headed. The apostle John said, *"Jesus knew that the Father had put all things under His power, and that*

He had come from God and was returning to God" (John 13:3 NIV). According to the biblical account, at dinner one evening just a few days before Jesus' death, He dressed Himself like one of the servants and washed His disciples' feet. That would be like the President of the United States getting up from the table to take out the garbage at a White House banquet. But Jesus, the Lord of the Universe, was able to humble Himself this way because He knew that very soon He would be back in Heaven ruling the universe with His Father.

Time and time again Jesus amazed even His enemies with His knowledge and comprehension of the Scriptures. How else could He have "resolutely set out for Jerusalem," knowing the abuse and type of death that awaited Him? (See Isaiah 50:7 and Luke 9:51.)

He told His followers that if they *lived according to* His teaching, they would prove to the world that they *truly believed* His teachings. "If you hold to My teaching," He said to them, *"you are really My disciples. Then you will know the truth, and the truth will set you free"* (John 8:32 NIV).

By learning the Word of God, trusting in it, and holding to it, you can replace your incorrect judgments with true ones. This is what the apostle Paul meant when he said, *"Do not conform any longer to the pattern of this world, but be transformed by the renewing of your mind"* (Rom. 12:2 NIV).

Many of us function within a value system that has been conformed to the pattern of this world. But we need to transform these values according to the Word of God. Paul describes the sanctification of the entire Church in terms of changing our thinking to conform to the Word of God, *"cleansing her by the washing with water through the word"* (Eph. 5:26 NIV).

Are you willing to lay aside your long-held conclusions about life when God's Word teaches otherwise about a matter? If you are, then turn the key and start your car with the following principles from the trustworthy Word. Make them real in your life.

Replace Vows With Truth

In Psalm 119:98-100, the psalmist says:

> *Your commands make me wiser than my enemies, for they are ever with me. I have more insight than all my teachers, for I meditate on Your statutes. I have more understanding than the elders, for I obey Your precepts.*

Both the Old Testament and the New attest to the fact that people acquire Truth by knowing and obeying the Word of God. If you have not begun that process, please begin right here—do not let your judgments about God's Word cause you to reject this teaching. Choose to let the Word of God have dominion within your value system. This is the *beginning point*. It's "square one." If you cannot get past this point, *then you will remain stuck where you are until you do.*

So what does the Word of God say about trusting God? Psalm 103:2 (NIV) says, *"Praise the Lord, O my soul, and forget not all His benefits."* Trusting God results in many benefits (such as peace that passes understanding, unspeakable joy, friendship with God, and many more that are enumerated throughout the Bible) that should never be forgotten. They are all available to you, but there is a catch: *You must first trust in Him in order to receive them.*

Paul wanted the believers at Corinth to understand this idea when he wrote to them about the Old Testament record of Israel's history. He wrote, *"These things happened to them as examples and were written down as warnings for us, on whom the fulfillment of the ages has come"* (1 Cor. 10:11 NIV).

So then, learn from the Old Testament; it exists for your benefit. In 1887, hymn writer John H. Sammis penned these simple words that express a profound truth about trusting in God for all areas of your life: "Trust and obey, for there's no other way to be happy in Jesus, but to trust and obey."

Trusting God Is a Sacrifice

You must first realize that trusting requires making a sacrifice. David, the psalm-writing shepherd boy who slew Goliath, was chosen by God to replace Saul as king of Israel. Why? What was wrong with God's first choice, the tall and handsome Saul?

After Saul had been king for some time, he brought his army to Gilgal to fight the Philistines. He had been instructed to wait there seven days for the arrival of the prophet Samuel, who was supposed to offer a sacrifice to the Lord. But Samuel was slow in coming, and Saul's men, already fearful of the Philistines, began to scatter. So Saul took matters into his own hands and offered the sacrifice himself. Just as he finished, Samuel arrived and told Saul that his impulsive, foolish actions had cost him the kingdom. Moreover, Samuel continued, God had sought out another man to be king, *"a man after His own heart"* (1 Sam. 13:14).

That man, though still a boy at the time, was the same David who would later slay the giant Goliath. David understood that God wasn't interested in sacrifices offered out of fear and disobedience, as were Saul's. And David wrote, *"Offer the sacrifices of righteousness, and trust in the Lord"* (Ps. 4:5).

Sacrifice requires giving up or putting to death something that is valuable to us. It isn't easy. It isn't supposed to be. Otherwise, where would the sacrifice be? In a similar sacrificial way, it isn't easy to trust. When we initially trust in God, we must sacrifice some of our prior beliefs. Gradually, trust becomes easier because we realize that we profit by our investment of trust in Him.

I (Alan) once counseled a woman I'll call "Meredith" who had an abusive husband, "Ronald." As we talked about what had to change in her life, Meredith realized that she needed to protect herself with better emotional boundaries. In the past, when Ronald had verbally and sexually abused her, Meredith had thought it wasn't his fault. She would blame herself.

In counseling, we talked about the truth that through Christ's death, Meredith had become a new creation (see 2 Cor. 5:17). As a child of God, she was cleansed from her old life of sin and now had a new identity. Gradually, Meredith realized that she needed to let go of her old picture of herself and allow herself to live as the new person she actually was in Christ.

This meant that Meredith had to do something so hard for her to do that she hated doing it: resist and assert herself against Ronald when he used and abused her for his own lust, rather than love. It took months for her to finally say no and prevent him from verbally and physically attacking her. She also had to say no to the "old tapes" in her head. It took months of meeting with some loving women on a weekly basis to learn to "tell herself the truth" and believe the Word of God rather than her thoughts. And it took meeting with a counselor to reaffirm what she was doing until she was healthy. She did something she hated doing in order to get something she loved—a healthy relationship with God.

Sometimes you have to do something you hate in order to get something you love.

Trusting God Releases His Power in Your Life

When Jesus offered the ultimate sacrifice of Himself on the Cross at Calvary, that sacrifice released greater power than the world had ever seen or will ever see again. Men were reconciled to God, and all the works of His enemy, the liar, were crushed. In fact, not only was the liar defeated, but the Bible says that all his cohorts, called "powers" and "authorities," were openly humiliated because they were so soundly beaten by Christ's sacrifice on the Cross (see Col. 2:15).

But how could that be, when Christ died, bloody and naked, such a torturous and humiliating death? The answer is that three days later, God displayed His Sovereign approval of that sacrifice as full payment for the sins of mankind by triumphing over death and raising Christ from the grave.

Because trust in God is a sacrifice, it releases His power in your life. A couple of easily overlooked verses in the Old Testament illustrate this principle, though you may have to do a bit of reading between the lines to catch it. This chapter in First Chronicles 5 could be called something like "The Further Adventures of Israel After They Entered the Promised Land." In the midst of a string of genealogies and names difficult to pronounce, the narrative describes the adventures of the descendants of Reuben and Gad (who were sons of Jacob, the father of the nation of Israel) and of Manasseh (one of Jacob's grandsons).[1] It says that they were able to form an army of 44,760 men who went to war against the Hagrites (who were some of the descendants of Ishmael)—in other words, they were distant relatives of the Israelites through their common forefather, Abraham. But they were bitter enemies.

Verse 20 of this little account holds the crucial information for our example of how God's power is activated by trust. It says, *"They* [that is, the Israelites] *were helped against them, and the Hagrites and all who were with them were given into their hand; for they* [that is, the Israelites] *cried out to God in the battle, and He answered their prayers because they **trusted** in Him"* (1 Chron. 5:20).

Trust is the key element needed to see the release of His power in your life. God has not changed; He will do the same for you if you trust in Him.

Trusting God Releases His Blessings and Goodness to You

Oh how great is Thy goodness, which Thou hast laid up for them that fear Thee; which Thou hast wrought for them that trust in Thee before the sons of men (Psalm 31:19 KJV).

O Lord of hosts, how blessed is the man who trusts in You (Psalm 84:12).

Can God say this more clearly? If you want to see the blessings of God, then trust in Him. As a child, you may have sung "God is so good," but many of us have never recognized His goodness in our lives. Trust releases that goodness to us.

Remember, this is part of the New Covenant; if you place your trust in God, then He promises to impart His goodness, which is stored up for you. It is nothing that you earn, but is a gift from Him released by your trust. On the other hand, if you withhold your trust from God, then your mistrust will block His blessings and goodness.

Trusting God Releases Victory to Your Life by Establishing You in Conflicts

Another Old Testament story, told in Second Chronicles chapter 20, contains an example for us. Please take a few minutes to read and meditate upon it before continuing.

This story describes another occasion in which Israelite warriors had to go to battle against an alliance of their enemies. At this point in Israel's history, the nation had split into two kingdoms. Jehoshaphat was king over the southern kingdom of Judah, and the three nations of Ammon, Moab, and Mount Seir (the Edomites, descendants of Esau previously mentioned in Chapter 4) had allied against them. Jehoshaphat received news of their planned invasion and, in his fear, did what any good king of Israel should do. According to verse 3, he *"turned his attention to seek the Lord, and proclaimed a fast throughout all Judah"* (2 Chron. 20:3).

During the ensuing prayer rally, Jehoshaphat cried out to God, reminding Him of His promises and faithfulness in the past. Then one of the Levites—a tribe that had been set apart by God to serve Him in His temple—was inspired by God to proclaim that God was promising them victory. Filled with gratitude, Jehoshaphat fell on his face and worshiped.

Early the next morning, Jehoshaphat acted on his faith and led his army out to face their enemies. The Scripture says that he:

> *...stood and said, "Listen to me, O Judah and inhabitants of Jerusalem, put your trust in the Lord your God, and you will be established. Put your trust in His prophets and succeed."*
> *...When they began singing and praising, the Lord set ambushes against the sons of Ammon, Moab and Mount Seir, who*

had come against Judah, so they were routed (2 Chronicles 20:20,22).

The Lord had put it into the evil hearts of the Ammonites and the Moabites to attack their allies, the troops from Seir. Then they turned on one another. When the men of Judah arrived at the battlefield, it was full of their enemies' corpses.

Because they trusted in God, Jehoshaphat and the men of Judah were established in the land rather than destroyed; they had victory rather than defeat; and they brought home material blessings to their families from the spoils of the battle.

This story teaches us that God establishes us in conflict situations when we put our trust in Him. In this case, the Lord completely handled the problem for the people of Judah. The battle they had initially feared never even occurred.

In facing conflicts in your life, the difficult part is the mental preparation for the confrontation as much as, or even more than, the actual fight itself. Overcoming your own fear presents the greatest struggle. Once you make the decision to act and begin to proceed, you have put the hard part behind you. Your trust in God is demonstrated by your actions.

Trusting God Creates Inner Joy and Brings Happiness to Your Life

Even though your life may be filled with sorrows and suffering, trusting in God brings you joy. Inherent in the choice to trust in God is the choice to be joyful and to have faith in Him to overcome any situation. God wants your emotional status to be dictated by your relationship to Him, and not by situations in your life. You can take control of your emotional well-being by trusting in God.

In a psalm that reiterates the lesson we learned from Jehoshaphat, the psalmist says:

> *The king is not saved by a mighty army; a warrior is not delivered by great strength. ...Behold the eye of the Lord is on those*

who fear Him, on those who hope for His loving kindness.
...Our soul waits for the Lord; He is our help and our shield.
For our heart rejoices in Him, because we trust in His holy
name (Psalm 33:16,18,20-21).

Most people want to be happy. But happiness is based on happenings—in other words, on our circumstances. We Americans grow up believing that we have the right to life, liberty, and the pursuit of happiness, but the liar has stolen these things from us and in return has given us death, bondage to sin, and sometimes more misery than we can handle. By trusting in Jesus, we have eternal *life, liberty* from our bondage to sin, and a much more permanent version of *happiness*. As hard as we may try, we will not find real, lasting happiness anywhere else other than trusting in God.

In Proverbs 28:25, Solomon teaches, *"An arrogant man stirs up strife, but he who trusts in the Lord will prosper."* Although it's not a necessary ingredient for happiness, prosperity can be one of trust's fringe benefits. During the last couple of decades, many teachings on prosperity have gone to extremes, as though God owes each of us a small fortune; still Scripture does assert that God will bless those who live according to His Word.

Note that trusting in the Lord is here contrasted with being arrogant (or too proud to trust the Lord) and thereby creating strife. This verse states that the Lord *will* prosper those who trust in Him. It is your choice whether to believe the critics and embrace poverty or to trust in God and prosper.

Another Scripture passage with a promise begins and ends with trust:

> *Trust in the Lord, and do good; dwell in the land and cultivate*
> *faithfulness. Delight yourself in the Lord; and He will give you*
> *the desires of your heart. Commit your way to the Lord, trust*
> *also in Him, and He will do it* (Psalm 37:3-5).

What are the desires of your heart? Their fulfillment depends upon your level of trust in God. Jesus commanded, *"Trust in God, trust also in Me"* (John 14:1 NIV). Jesus did not intend for trust to be optional.

Trusting God Produces Endurance in Your Life and Preserves You in Hard Times

Few persons have experienced misfortunes such as Job's. In the course of a day, he lost all of his material wealth and all of his children through the supernatural interference of satan, the liar. When Job continued to remain faithful to the Lord despite his circumstance, the liar petitioned the Lord for permission to smite Job with itchy, ugly boils. Throughout his ordeal, Job remained faithful to the Lord.

We have the benefit of hindsight in analyzing why these things happened, but Job had to endure this without ever knowing why. His endurance was established through his trust and hope in God. I (Ed) urge you to maintain your trust in God during adversity. It will give you the endurance you need to overcome.

Years ago, Alan and Pauly traveled to a small town in New England to visit college friends with whom they had a long conversation about spiritual things. Looking for a Christian bookstore where they could buy a book for their friends, they were directed to a house on a side street, where they'd been told a store was opening. An elderly woman responded to their knock by welcoming them into a room filled with boxes of books.

The woman—we'll call her Lucinda because Pauly doesn't remember her name—was surprised that anyone knew about her store because it wasn't open yet. Nevertheless, she had a copy of the book they were looking for. As they chatted, Lucinda told them that she had always loved the Lord and known she wanted to serve Him. On the day she graduated from high school, Lucinda received a vision from the Lord. In her vision, the Lord told her something like, "Lucinda, I know you love Me and want to serve Me. So I'm giving you a choice for your life. I have chosen you for much suffering. You have a choice to refuse this purpose, and I will still love you. But if you agree, your life will bring Me much glory."

Lucinda went on to list the many trials that had come her way in her 80 years of life—things like debilitating illness, countless hospitalizations, temporary blindness, and near-death experiences. Her husband had spent many years of his life as an invalid, and Lucinda had cared for him as well. But rather than griping about her bad luck and the unfairness of it all, she glowed with the presence of the Lord within her and couldn't say enough about His great love for her and us.

Psalm 16:1 (KJV) says, *"Preserve me, O God: for in Thee do I put my trust."* There are many other ways to gain endurance besides trusting in God, but endurance does not guarantee our preservation through a difficult time. Trust does! Our trust in God not only produces endurance, but it also preserves us in our trials.

Trusting God Releases His Loving-kindness Toward You

Most of us are familiar with the story of young David's mighty slingshot victory over gargantuan Goliath. And many have heard of his lustful indiscretion with Bathsheba, his neighbor's wife. But some of you may not be as familiar with some of David's other adventures. For instance, learning that David would be replacing him as king, Saul tried on more than one occasion to kill him. David and some faithful followers were forced to hide from Saul in Israel's hill country, often camping out in caves. Twice David had the opportunity to kill his relentless pursuer, but he refused to murder God's anointed king. Yet Saul "rewarded" David's faithfulness with renewed vengeance, forcing David to seek refuge among his enemies, the Philistines.

Furthermore, after he became king of Israel, David fought in countless battles to secure Israel's peace and ultimate prosperity. In all these hardships and adversities, David remained steadfast in his trust in God.[2] The following is a portion of one of his recorded prayers:

*My steps have held to Your paths; my feet have not slipped. I call on You, O God, for You will answer me; give ear to me and hear my prayer. Show the wonder of **Your great love**, You who save by Your right hand those who take refuge in You from their foes (Psalm 17:5-7 NIV).*

You'll never catch David pouting or blaming God for his trials in life. But that doesn't mean that he never complained to God about them. Indeed his psalms often give the Lord an earful about the strain of eluding those who continually sought to kill him—including his own son, Absalom. But in the midst of all those complaints, David resolved, *"that my mouth will not sin"* (Ps. 17:3 NIV).

Yes, David often found himself in treacherous and life-threatening circumstances, but he recognized those circumstances as opportunities for God to rescue him and to *"show the wonder of* [His] *great love."* David's very name means "beloved of God," though few of our Bible heroes endured more trials than he did. Yet he was able to say, *"Thy loving kindness is better than life."*

The Bible tells us that you cannot please God without faith (see Heb. 11:6). Faith begins with trust. You must first trust God to be who He says He is before you can act on His Word in faith. Then you will get to witness the wonder of His great love. And He will save you by His *right hand*—the Old Testament symbolic term for the Messiah—as you show your trust by taking refuge in Him during your trials.

Trusting God Stops You From Seeking After Idols in Your Life

In the first and second of the Ten Commandments, God says:

> *You shall have no other gods before Me. You shall not make for yourself an idol in the form of anything in heaven above or on the earth beneath or in the waters below. You shall not bow down to them or worship them; for I, the Lord your God, am a jealous God, punishing the children to the third and fourth generation of those who hate Me, but showing love to a thousand generations of those who love Me and keep My commandments* (Exodus 20:3-6 NIV).

Another of David's psalms contains the bold proclamation, *"I hate those who cling to worthless idols; I trust in the Lord"* (Ps. 31:6 NIV). As a young, idealistic Jewish girl, I (Pauly) often wondered how anyone would be foolish enough to believe in idols. How could anyone possibly think an inanimate statue would be able to do anything for him? Especially when an all-powerful God, who split the sea for the Israelites and brought them to the Promised Land, reigned supreme in the heavens.

Then I grew up.

I wanted to be beautiful, but I wasn't. I wanted to be rich, but I wasn't. I wanted to be famous, but I certainly wasn't that, either. And I wanted to marry a husband who would be handsome, rich, and famous and provide for me everything I wanted in life. In fact, most of what I wanted fell into a materialistic range of items that I thought were guaranteed to make me feel secure and happy.

True, some followers of certain religions offer food, money, incense, and other sacrifices before statues representing their gods. But in our industrialized, materialistic Western culture, our idols are more sophisticated. Nevertheless, whatever form they take, idols are merely those things that the liar offers us as substitutes for the invisible, one true God. The liar says, "Why put your trust in something you can't even see? How do you know He, She, or It (another huge lie) is even there? Now here's something real, something tangible, something you can sink your teeth into. Put your trust in this business opportunity...cosmetic surgery...investment plan...addictive behavior...political leader instead." The liar never overtly calls this thing an idol. He just directs our attention away from the True God so we put our trust in something that will never deliver what it promises.

By trusting in the True God who will never fail us, we will not be tempted to place our trust in worthless idols. Christian counselor Larry Crabb says that such behavior is "meeting legitimate needs in an illegitimate way."

Trusting God Delivers You From the Wicked

We've already described David's frequent escapes from the murderous hand of King Saul and how David refused to retaliate when given the opportunity. He wrote in the Psalms:

> *And the Lord shall help them, and deliver them: He shall deliver them from the wicked, and save them, because they trust in Him* (Psalm 37:40 KJV).

And:

> *O my God, in You I trust, do not let me be ashamed; do not let my enemies exult over me* (Psalm 25:2).

David chose not to fear Saul and his army because he knew that God was faithful to complete the work He began when Samuel anointed him king of Israel. David knew that one of God's attributes is faithfulness. He always finishes what He starts. The apostle Paul reminded his friends at Philippi of this quality when he wrote to them that they could be confident that *"He who began a good work in you will carry it on **to completion** until the day of Christ Jesus"* (Phil. 1:6 NIV).

So not only do we have God's promise that He will finish the work of faith that He began in us until we are "complete," or fully mature—which will occur when we leave this life and go to live with Him in Christ in His eternal Heaven—but we have His promise of victory over the liar. The apostle John encourages us with these words: *"You, dear children, are from God and have overcome them* [that is, evil spirits]*, because the one who is in you is greater than the one who is in the world"* (1 John 4:4 NIV).

Live your life *free from fear*. Trust in the Lord. He will lift you up and banish your shame as He brings you victory and safety.

Trust Brings God's Help in Times of Sorrow

> *Many are the sorrows of the wicked; but he who trusts in the Lord, loving kindness shall surround him* (Psalm 32:10).

Nowhere in Scripture are we assured a life free from sorrow and trouble. In fact, in His final conversation with His disciples prior to His arrest and crucifixion, Jesus foretold, *"In this world you will have trouble."* But with this grim prophecy, the Messiah promised His encouragement and ultimate victory, saying, *"But take heart! I have overcome the world"* (John 16:33 NIV).

One of our fundamental beliefs as Christians is that Christ will be "formed in us" (see Gal. 4:19). So then, should we expect a life without sorrows when Jesus Himself was called *"a man of sorrows, and familiar with suffering"* (Isa. 53:3 NIV)? What we need in order to endure through such times is the loving-kindness and compassion of God. It is ours if we will put our trust in God.

Furthermore, Paul says, *"We **know** that all things work together for the good of those that love Him..."* (see Rom. 8:28). When we truly trust in God, we know and trust the truth of this promise. We trust in God's sovereignty in our lives; that He really does love us and has benevolent plans for us; that He sees the big picture while we are shortsighted; that even pain and suffering in our lives will produce good fruit in His time; and that this promise to Jesus will also apply to us: *"He shall see the fruit of the travail of His soul and be satisfied"* (Isa. 53:11 RSV).

ENDNOTES

1. This Joseph is not to be confused with the husband of Mary, Jesus' mother, but is the favorite son of Jacob, whose brothers sold him into slavery in Egypt, where he interpreted Pharaoh's dreams and saved Egypt from a ravaging famine.

2. The life of David and his conflict with Saul are recorded in the Book of First Samuel.

CHAPTER 10

Don't Adjust It — Trust It:
More of God's Word on Trust

"Pleasing God is actually a by-product of trusting God."

—Bill Thrall[1]

⟐

My (Alan's) friend Mike said to me, "People will let you down, but God will never let you down." Through my years of walking with the Lord, He has also proved over and over again that His Word will never let me down either. Below are six more reasons why you can rely on every word in that Word:

Trusting God Produces a Spirit-led, Spirit-bred, and Spirit-fed Life

Many of David's psalms contrast various aspects of wicked men and their resultant destruction with the opposing qualities and blessings of faithful people. In Psalm 52, he describes evil people as those who boast about all their various forms of wickedness.

Hurricane Katrina afforded us graphic images of the destruction of the city of New Orleans by gales that lifted entire buildings off their foundations, shredding their bricks and steel girders like so many birds' nests in the wind. This is the picture that David paints of God snatching up and tearing the wicked from their tents, uprooting them from the land of the living (see Ps. 52:5).

By contrast, David rejoices about the hope of the righteous, singing, *"I am like an olive tree flourishing in the house of God; I trust in God's unfailing love for ever and ever"* (Ps. 52:8 NIV).

A green olive tree in the house of God is well-fertilized, well-watered, regularly trimmed, basks in the radiant sunshine of God's presence, and always bears its fruit, out of which is pressed the oil of the Holy Spirit. We are planted by God (Spirit-bred), nourished by God (Spirit-fed), and always do the will of God (Spirit-led). This lifestyle begins with trusting in God.

Trusting God Draws You Near to God

"I will abide in Thy tabernacle forever: I will trust in the covert of Thy wings" (Ps. 61:4 KJV). With these words, David echoes Moses' narrative song—sung to all the nation of Israel as they stood at the end of their wilderness wanderings ready to enter the Promised Land. Moses told them:

> *Oh, praise the greatness of our God! He is the Rock, His works are perfect, and all His ways are just…. In a desert land He found [Jacob], in a barren and howling waste. He shielded him and cared for him; He guarded him as the apple of His eye, like an eagle that stirs up its nest and hovers over its young, that spreads its wings to catch them and carries them on its pinions. The Lord alone led him* (Deuteronomy 32:3-4, 10-12 NIV).

Do you see the picture of God's nurturing care? He saw Jacob when he was just a guy on the lam, who'd cheated his older brother out of birthright and blessing and was running scared for his life. God watched over him and protected him and provided for him and blessed him in spite of himself. Twelve sons, 400 years in Egypt, and

40 years in the wilderness later, Jacob had grown into the mighty nation of Israel, poised to claim the land God had promised to them.

Now David, in Psalm 61, recalls Moses' imagery: the *"rock that is higher than I"* and the *"shelter of Your wings."* Where are this rock and those wings to be found? These are figurative representations of God's tabernacle—His appointed place of worship.

Do you want to draw near to God? There is nothing that compares to knowing that you are close to God, feeling His love and protection. Trust in the Lord to protect you; take refuge in the shelter of His wings. It is your choice to abide in His tabernacle. It begins with trust.

Trusting God Gives You Courage to Declare His Works

The apostle Paul, the greatest evangelist of all time, admitted in a letter to the church at Corinth, "I came to you in weakness and fear, and with much trembling." After all, Paul was human too, and he never knew how listeners would receive his Gospel message—with open hearts or with ostracism. But before he even entered their city, he *"resolved to know nothing while* [he] *was with* [them] *except Jesus Christ and Him crucified"* (1 Cor. 2:2 NIV).

An expert in the Hebrew Old Testament Scriptures, Paul certainly not only knew but experienced firsthand the truth of Psalm 73:28: *"But as for me, the nearness of God is my good; I have made the Lord God my refuge, that I may tell of all Your works."*

Fear can keep you from declaring the Kingdom of God as you may desire. But by making God your refuge and drawing near to Him, fear of rejection will be driven out. Put your trust in God, and the fruit of this trust will be that fear flees. Then you'll be able to declare the works of the Lord to all those around you.

Trusting God Helps You to Take Courage

What an inspiration and example David is to us! His life reads like a television action-adventure series in which the hero is placed in life-threatening situations week after week. Yet David's life was no

Hollywood scriptwriter's creation; he was a true hero of the faith who beat the odds time and time again because he relied on God to pull him through seemingly impossible calamities.

David wrote Psalm 56 to commemorate such a time when the Philistines captured him in Gath, Goliath's home country. There he was—surrounded by the giant race of people whose hero he had toppled with a well-placed stone to the forehead. What were David's odds of survival in that setting? It's kind of reminiscent of cartoons depicting a hunter tied up in a pot over a fire surrounded by cannibals.

But what does David say here? *"In God I have put my trust, I shall not be afraid. What can man do to me?"* (Ps. 56:11).

The apostle Paul said, *"If God is for us who can be against us?"* (Rom. 8:31 NIV). Having our trust in God instills us with complete courage in any situation. Someone who opposes us is opposing God. How dare we feel fearful of any situation when we have placed our trust in God? Trust in God and fear are opposite states of mind.

Trusting God Overcomes the Negative Effects of Uncertainty

Trust in the Lord with all your heart, and do not lean on your own understanding. In all your ways acknowledge Him, and He will make your paths straight (Proverbs 3:5-6).

God is in control; He is guiding you through life's maze of circumstances and attendant decisions that must be made along the way. Don't know which career to choose? Which man (or woman) to marry? Whether or not to buy a particular house? How to discipline your children?

Do you think your problems are too small for God to concern Himself with them? Take heart from these words of Jesus: *"Are not two sparrows sold for a penny? Yet not one of them will fall to the ground apart from the will of your Father. And even the very hairs of your head are all numbered. So don't be afraid; you are worth more than many sparrows"* (Matt. 10:29-31 NIV). If the very hairs of our head are numbered, don't you think that God may even have a plan for your life?

The God who created you, who chose and formed your personality, gave you an intellect, who determined the dimensions and structure of your body—He has prepared a work for you that will challenge you, reward you, and give you a fulfilling life. He has not prepared a dead-end job and poverty for your future. You will find His will for your life by trusting in Him with all of your heart!

Trusting God Keeps You in a Safe Place

Wise King Solomon wrote, *"Fearing people is a dangerous trap, but to trust the Lord means safety"* (Prov. 29:25 NLT).

It's only natural to be concerned with what other people think about you. However, the person who trusts in God is more concerned about what God thinks; he is not swayed by public opinion. Many of the Jewish people in Jesus' day were kept from entering God's Kingdom because their fear of men exceeded their fear of God.

Yet at the same time, many even among the leaders believed in Him. However, they would not confess their faith for fear that the Pharisees—who were powerful and influential religious leaders—would put them out of the synagogue. In other words, *"they loved praise from men more than praise from God"* (John 12:42-43 NIV).

Don't let fear of losing face before your friends and acquaintances disqualify you from the Kingdom or rob you of its benefits. Trusting in God often requires believers to act contrary to popular opinion. People love to exalt themselves in the sight of others but Jesus said, *"Whoever exalts himself will be humbled, and whoever humbles himself will be exalted"* (Matt. 23:12 NIV).

Be obedient to the Lord and trust in Him by humbling yourself. Show deference to others and honor them by being their servant. Ask yourself this question: Where is it that I want to be exalted, in this world or in the Kingdom of God? Put your trust in God and act accordingly.

A Final Word on Trust

Meditate on these Scripture truths. Let them sink in and become part of your reasoning process. Reject your old beliefs that contradict what God says. Remember Psalm 12:6 (NIV), "*And the words of the Lord are flawless, like silver refined in a furnace of clay, purified seven times.*" Hold to these teachings; then you will know the truth about trusting God and this truth will set you free from the limitations of your own self-reliance.

> *Praise the Lord, O my soul; all my inmost being, praise His holy name. Praise the Lord, O my soul, and forget not all His benefits—who forgives all your sins and heals all your diseases, who redeems your life from the pit and crowns you with love and compassion, who satisfies your desires with good things so that your youth is renewed like the eagle's* (Psalm 103:1-5 NIV).

Remember:

1. Replace vows with Truth.
2. Trusting God is a sacrifice.
3. Trusting God releases His power in your life.
4. Trusting God releases His blessings and goodness to you.
5. Trusting God releases victory to your life by establishing you in conflicts.
6. Trusting God creates inner joy and brings happiness to your life.
7. Trusting God produces endurance in your life and preserves you in hard times.
8. Trusting God releases His loving-kindness toward you.
9. Trusting God stops you from seeking after idols in your life.
10. Trusting God delivers you from the wicked.
11. Trusting brings God's help in times of sorrow.
12. Trusting God produces a Spirit-led, Spirit-bred, and Spirit-fed life.
13. Trusting God draws you near to God.
14. Trusting God gives you courage to declare His works.
15. Trusting God helps you to take courage.

16. Trusting God overcomes the negative effects of uncertainty.

17. Trusting God keeps you in a safe place.

If you have trouble remembering these 17 points, you may condense their ideas into one simple motto: "Don't adjust it; trust it!"

ENDNOTE

1. Bill Thrall, Bruce McNicol, and John Lynch, *TrueFaced: Trust God and Others With Who You Really Are* (Colorado Springs, CO: Navpress, 2004), 44.

CHAPTER II

Trust Traps — Who and What Not to Trust

*For it is inevitable that
stumbling blocks come...*
(Matthew 18:7).

The Bible names specific things in which you are not supposed to trust. The liar relentlessly attempts to convince you to place your trust in these idols. Destined to fail you, these idols will ensnare you in the liar's Anti-Trust Strategy.

Idols and Gods

God's Word enumerates His contempt for idols. The following passage from Psalms vividly depicts their nature and pitiful limitations as well as the consequences of trusting in them:

The idols of the nations are silver and gold, made by the hands of men. They have mouths, but cannot speak, eyes, but they cannot see; they have ears, but cannot hear, nor is there breath in their mouths. Those who make them will be like them, and so will all who trust in them (Psalm 135:15-18 NIV).

Notice four things God says about an idol's abilities (or lack thereof):

1. It has a mouth but is unable to speak the wisdom of God or give any advice in a tough situation.
2. Its eyes cannot see the problems you experience.
3. Its ears cannot hear your prayers, praise, and petitions.
4. It doesn't have the breath of life that might possibly enable it to act on your behalf.

Any person or thing that you make into an idol (God's impostor) by giving it your admiration and devotion will have these same shortcomings. It's no wonder that your idols fail you when you turn to them in a time of need. *It is impossible for an idol to do anything but fail you!* Whatever or whomever you idolize will disappoint you sooner or later, and if satan, the liar, can help it, this disappointment will come to you at a critical time.

The prophet Isaiah wrote, *"But those who trust in idols, who say to images, 'You are our gods,' will be turned back in utter shame"* (Isa. 42:17 NIV). Idols will shame you when you place your trust in them.

A friend of mine was driving across town one fine spring day, and saw in his rear-view mirror a red convertible rapidly overtaking him. My friend held his speed, staying in his lane so the red car could pass safely, and then watched as it wove in and out of traffic at 25 miles per hour above the speed limit. Seconds later and several blocks ahead, the red car's driver lost control trying to avoid a slow-moving vehicle that was hindering his reckless forward progress. The red car skidded sideways onto the sidewalk, wrapping its passenger door around a large steel pole. As my friend drove by, he looked at the red car's lone occupant, a young man sitting unhurt in the driver's seat. His face wore an expression of total humiliation as he avoided eye contact with my friend and all the other drivers now passing him. His idols—"incredibly fast, unbeatable, road-hugging, red racing machine" and "cat-like reflexes and superior driving skills"—had failed him, and everyone driving past knew it.

God reprimanded His people about their idolatry through the prophet Isaiah, saying, *"When you cry out for help, let your collection of idols save you! The wind will carry all of them off, a mere breath will blow them away. But the man who makes Me his refuge will inherit the land and possess My holy mountain"* (Isa. 57:13 NIV).

Likewise, the prophet Jeremiah points out the futility of trusting in anything other than God: *"Do any of the worthless idols of the nations bring rain? Do the skies themselves send down showers? No, it is You, O Lord our God. Therefore our hope is in You, for You are the one who does all this"* (Jer. 14:22 NIV).

When the ramifications of trusting in idols are so devastating and the blessings of trusting God are so secure, why do we so often foolishly choose to trust our idols? We are deceived into making this asinine (ill-considered) decision by the liar. He tells us the opposite of what God's Word tells us, and does it in such a way that we accept the lie as the truth! Usually it is not until the idol has disappointed us that we begin to question why we "got burned" again.

Have you been deceived into trusting in something (or someone) other than God? *Recognize, remove, and replace that idol with Almighty God—the only one worthy of trust.*

Beauty or Good Looks

The prophet Ezekiel penned an allegory that compared Jerusalem, the capital city of the Jewish nation, to an adulterous wife who prostituted herself. *"But you trusted in your beauty and used your fame to become a prostitute,"* he wrote (Ezek. 16:15 NIV).

We live in a society whose mass media persuades us that we need to be beautiful (or handsome) and that wonderful things will happen to our lives if we will buy the products they advertise. Although we recognize the lies in these sales pitches, we hear and see them so often that they subtly persuade us through their repetition. These deceptions are difficult to overcome. They're part of the spirit of *"this present evil age"* (Gal. 1:4).

The false value system created by an emphasis on physical appearance is especially difficult for someone who is considered beautiful. Remember the evil queen in Snow White? "Mirror, mirror, on the wall, who's the fairest of them all?" When the mirror revealed someone more beautiful than she, it threw her into an emotional tailspin. Snow White threatened the queen's significance, acceptance, security, and love. When this type of thinking reaches the stronghold stage, we encounter problems like bulimia, anorexia, anabolic steroid abuse, and a host of other self-destructive behaviors.

God never intended that you trust in your superficial looks, but that you trust in Him. God doesn't love you for your outward beauty, but rather for who you are! Isn't that what you desire from other people with whom you have relationships?

Man-made Weapons for War

Forty-two percent of American homes contain at least one gun. In the name of self-defense, many women, who have traditionally shied away from gun use and ownership, have begun carrying weapons in order to feel more secure. Many of my (Ed's) neighbors go for their evening strolls around the block armed with either a gun or a club. I'm not anti-gun-ownership, but leaning on weapons rather than on God is a form of idolatry. When we trust our weapons rather than God for our safety, we are headed for trouble.

This self-defensive behavior has been fueled by the fear of crime, even though statistics show that overall crime in this country has actually decreased per capita.[1] Americans have always loved their guns—the more powerful, the better. They provide a feeling of power. As a nation, we have one of the largest and most effective military establishments in the world. Yet, the issue of cutting defense spending incites some of the most heated debates within Congress. What does God's Word say about such self-reliance?

For I will not trust in my bow, nor will my sword save me (Psalm 44:6).

The Lord is the only one you can trust to protect you and your family in every situation and at all times. The ability of your weapons to protect you is limited by your own skills. Even David, Israel's valiant military hero and king, proclaimed that his abilities were made possible by the Lord. He did not trust in his own abilities or weapons to protect his life, but trusted in God, saying, *"Even though I walk through the valley of the shadow of death, I will fear no evil, for You are with me; Your rod and Your staff, they comfort me"* (Ps. 23:4 NIV).

I have also observed another danger about weaponry: Many individuals I have known have become totally obsessed with guns. I have asked myself, "What causes this obsession?"

A friend of mine told me of an electrical engineer with whom he worked who invited him to his apartment for dinner. At one point in the evening, he asked my friend if he wanted to see his machine-gun. My friend hesitantly said, "Sure." The engineer produced a military-style fully automatic weapon from beneath a sofa cushion (which, incidentally, concealed several more guns). The proud gun owner set up a stack of phone books in the corner and proceeded to fire a burst as my friend watched, dumbfounded. He declined the engineer's offer to fire the gun.

In this country, that type of man is not as unusual as you might think. I have known others who owned not just a few guns, but hundreds. These people are obsessed, not wanting to talk about anything else or do any other leisure activities but go shooting. Their guns give them a sense of power; machine guns seem to especially attract them.

I am persuaded that an addictive spirit is at work in their lives. That spirit will attempt to seduce anyone who begins to show too much interest in the ownership and use of weapons. *Guns make wonderful servants but terrible masters.*

King David fell into this trap when he allowed the liar to persuade him to take a census of his troops so he could know how powerful his army was. Even Joab, David's unrighteous general, tried to dissuade him from displaying such apparent lack of trust in God. The Lord's anger flared against David for focusing on his own military strength instead of trusting God's ability to conquer Israel's foes (see 1 Chron. 21).

Trust the Lord for your safety. Don't rely on man-made weapons alone for your security. Take heed of God's warning concerning those who trust in anyone or anything other than the Lord for their well-being:

> *Woe to those who go down to Egypt for help, who rely on horses, who trust in the multitude of their chariots and in the great strength of their horsemen, but do not look to the Holy One of Israel, or seek help from the Lord* (Isaiah 31:1 NIV).

Oppression of Men for Riches or Unrighteous Monetary Gain

I wish I didn't have to say anything about this subject, but some people have made money into an idol and are easily seduced by its lure.

In a psalm extolling God as his fortress and deliverer, David makes an astute observation about the advantages of wealth as opposed to the disadvantages of poverty. He says, *"Lowborn men are but a breath, the highborn are but a lie; if weighed on a balance, they are nothing; together they are only a breath"* (Ps. 62:9 NIV). In other words, these earthly measures of value bear no weight on Heaven's eternal scales. All the gold a rich man may possess doesn't weigh any more than a feather in eternity. So he continues, *"Do not trust in extortion or take pride in stolen goods; though your riches increase, do not set your heart on them"* (Ps. 62:10 NIV).

Examine all of your financial dealings with others and ask God to show you if there is anything of which He disapproves. If necessary, repent and make things right. Then learn what God's Word has to say about business and financial management, and put His principles into practice.

Lying or Cheating

Isaiah wrote, *"No one sues righteously and no one pleads honestly. They trust in confusion and speak lies; they conceive mischief and bring forth iniquity"* (Isa. 59:4).

Because we're writing predominantly to people who call themselves Christians, I like to think I shouldn't have to say much about this issue. However, many individuals make it a regular practice to deal less than honestly in their financial transactions with agencies such as the IRS. But Jesus made it clear that He expects His followers to be above reproach in all they do, not just in church-related activities. He taught, *"So in everything, do to others what you would have them do to you, for this sums up the Law and the Prophets"* (Matt. 7:12 NIV).

Just because a large agency like the IRS or an insurance company may have cheated or intimidated you, it does not give you license to "return the favor." The hand of the Lord will be against you if you place any trust in lying or cheating. Conduct all your business with total integrity.

Riches

To "trust in riches" means to trust your wealth for your future security. The Bible warns that your riches will fail and/or your life will fail. It says that riches cannot be trusted to always be there for you:

Cast but a glance at riches, and they are gone, for they will surely sprout wings and fly off to the sky like an eagle (Proverbs 23:5 NIV).

How many stories have you heard about someone who earned or inherited a great sum of money only to quickly lose it? A social worker in our city tells the story of a welfare recipient in the 1970s who won $20,000 in the state lottery and was back in the welfare office three weeks later asking for more assistance. For the first time in her life, this woman had a substantial amount of money. What happened to it? Why didn't she save or invest it?

People do not always use money wisely. Even for those who do make seemingly wise decisions with their money, the results are not always any better. After "Black Monday," the day of the 1987 stock market crash, a man killed his stockbroker and then himself because of his financial losses. Someone will always be seeking to separate you from your hard-earned money. For every dollar made in the stock market, someone loses a dollar. Unscrupulous savings-and-loan companies bilked thousands of people out of millions of dollars in the 1980s. These investments appeared sound initially, but turned to dust for those who had invested their life savings.

I (Ed) lost a substantial amount of money in a real estate investment recommended by my financial advisor. He, who also invested in it and had never steered me wrong in the past, presented it as a real moneymaker. Although the loss was disappointing, I knew that God was in control of the situation and, ultimately, in control of my future. You must learn to trust God for your future security and turn away from trusting in your own riches or financial wizardry.

Even if your investments don't turn sour, there is still no guarantee that you will be around to enjoy them. Jesus tells the story of a wealthy farmer who decided to build bigger barns to store his wealth and then retire:

> The ground of a certain rich man produced a good crop. He thought to himself, "What shall I do? I have no place to store my crops." Then he said, "This is what I'll do. I will tear down my barns and build bigger ones, and there I will store all my grain and my goods. And I'll say to myself, "You have plenty of good things laid up for many years. Take life easy; eat, drink and be merry."
>
> But God said to him, "You fool! This very night your life will be demanded from you. Then who will get what you have prepared for yourself?" This is how it will be with anyone who stores up things for himself but is not rich toward God (Luke 12:16-21 NIV).

In this story, Jesus implies that riches are not to be used for one's self but for others. Riches are a gift from God; they do have some specific uses, but your future security is not to be one of them. This man's life failed him and brought his trust in his riches to nothing.

Do not misunderstand what I am saying here. It is not wrong to save for the future or plan for your retirement. Money is a tool and must be used wisely. The point is this: Do not place your trust for future security in money. *Riches make wonderful servants but terrible masters!*

Depend on the Lord for your future. He is the one who gives you the ability to make plans for the future. Jesus said, *"But seek first His kingdom and His righteousness, and all these things will be given to you as well"* (Matt. 6:33 NIV).

Keep your priorities in order; place your trust in the Lord.

The Word also says, *"He who trusts in his riches will fall, but the righteous will flourish like the green leaf"* (Prov. 11:28). This verse implies that it is the unrighteous man who trusts in his own riches! Repent, therefore, from trusting in your own riches, your own financial genius, and your own abilities to create wealth. Trust only in the Lord.

Houses and Buildings

A home is the largest investment most people ever make; in most cases, it's a wise investment. However, you should never place your trust in the value of a home or any building. They are temporal, and can become idols to you. I watched with great sadness the Midwest flooding of 1993 and was deeply moved as some families lost everything they had worked so hard to accumulate. No matter how indestructible a home may seem, it is only a temporary dwelling place.

The Book of Job, the tale of the godly man who lost everything, says, *"He trusts in his house, but it does not stand; he holds fast to it, but it does not endure"* (Job 8:15).

A friend of mine, a pastor in California, related the story of one of his elders whose home was threatened by some nearby wildfires. My friend decided to stop by and encourage him and his family to trust that the Lord would keep them safe even though the fire was only a few hundred feet from their home. When he arrived, he found that they were completely distressed and inconsolable for fear of losing their home. "I learned that day," he said, "that they had not placed their trust in God."

Houses and buildings make wonderful servants but terrible masters!

Jews today still stand at the Wailing Wall in Jerusalem and mourn the loss of their temple, which was destroyed in A.D. 70.

> *Jesus left the temple and was walking away when His disciples came up to Him to call His attention to its buildings. "Do you see all these things?" He asked. "I tell you the truth, not one stone here will be left on another; every one will be thrown down"* (Matthew 24:1-2).

Notice that the disciples called Jesus' attention to the temple buildings. Perhaps they saw that Jesus did not seem quite as impressed with the buildings as they thought He should be. Surely, they thought, Jesus simply hasn't recognized the magnificence of the temple architecture and they needed to point it out to Him; then He would tell them wonderful things about the future of the temple in His coming Kingdom. I'm certain that they were speechless at Jesus' response. Not even the imposing edifice of God's magnificent golden temple was worthy of the disciples' trust; Jesus certainly did not place His trust in it.

Your Own Heart

> *He who trusts in his own heart is a fool, but he who walks wisely will be delivered* (Proverbs 28:26).

You cannot trust yourself any more than you can trust another person. The prophet Jeremiah wrote, *"The heart is deceitful above all things and beyond cure. Who can understand it?"* (Jer. 17:9 NIV). When guided by your soul and not the Spirit of God, your heart is fickle and has a tendency to sin. Unless the life of Christ is formed in you, your heart can be filled with all sorts of evil and cannot be trusted.

*"For out of the heart come evil thoughts, murder, adultery, sexual im-
morality, theft, false testimony, slander. These are what make a man 'un-
clean'"* (Matt. 15:19-20 NIV).

The area of your heart that will most often deceive you is your emotions. Many people make their decisions based on their emotions and
do not allow logic into the process—not to mention the Word of God.
The judgment/vow/generalization process generates emotions—such
as fear—to warn you not to trust. Little Albert felt fear, generated by
that process, whenever he was presented with a furry, white object.

A man came to me for counseling because he felt intense jealousy
at the mention of any of his wife's old boyfriends, even though she
had always been 100 percent loyal to him. During counseling, we
discovered that every girlfriend he'd had prior to his marriage had
left him for another man. He had overgeneralized the vows from
those painful memories, and they were generating unfounded fear.
When he understood what was happening, he was immediately set
free from that bondage of jealousy.

Emotions make wonderful servants but terrible masters!

Do not trust your emotions. They enrich your life, but they will
deceive you into making bad decisions.

Other People

*Do not trust in a neighbor; do not have confidence in a friend.
From her who lies in your bosom guard your lips* (Micah 7:5).

God's Word clearly commands us not to trust in friends and
neighbors. Paul never ministered or traveled alone, but was always
accompanied by other faithful men of God. Even so, he did not
place his trust in them (see 2 Cor. 1:9). Paul labored with men such
as Barnabas, Luke, Mark, Timothy, and Titus, yet he always placed
his trust in God, not in his companions.

*It is better to take refuge in the Lord than to trust in man. It
is better to take refuge in the Lord than to trust in princes*
(Psalm 118:8-9).

Our American culture maintains a pervasive mistrust of politicians. However, we still put the most prestigious names available to us on our résumés and drop names anytime we think it might benefit us. Most people in need of a favor will not hesitate to call upon someone in a powerful position. Put your trust in the Lord! He is the one who can really "pull strings" for you.

> *Thus says the Lord, "Cursed is the man who trusts in mankind and makes flesh his strength, and whose heart turns away from the Lord. For he will be like a bush in the desert and will not see when prosperity comes, but will live in stony wastes in the wilderness, a land of salt without inhabitant. Blessed is the man who trusts in the Lord and whose trust is the Lord"* (Jeremiah 17:5-7).

To put it bluntly, mankind in general is just not trustworthy. Trust in God who is able and willing to bless you.

Your Righteousness-based Self-effort

> *When I say to the righteous he will surely live, and he so trusts in his righteousness that he commits iniquity, none of his righteous deeds will be remembered; but in that same iniquity of his which he has committed he will die* (Ezekiel 33:13).

There are many religions and even Christian sects that emphasize the need for "good works" or "penance" as a necessary ingredient of salvation. This kind of thinking contradicts the teachings of salvation by faith through God's grace alone found in the Bible (see Eph. 2:8-9). Yet it has proliferated among the non-Christian population. When the subject of Heaven and hell is brought up, many people will respond, "I'm not a bad person." Yet your good works don't ensure that good things will always happen to you any more than they will ensure your entrance into Heaven.

What shall we say in response to this? Don't trust in:

- Idols and gods.
- Weapons.

- Oppression for gain.

- Lying or cheating.

- Riches.

- Houses.

- Your own heart.

- People.

- Self-effort.

When you trust in any of these things (or anything else that becomes an idol), you are falling into the liar's snare. Your idol will fail and the liar will persuade you to forsake trust in anything, especially in God.

ENDNOTE

1. U.S. Department of Justice–Office of Justice Program, Bureau of Justice Statistics says serious violent crime levels declined since 1993; after declining for many years, property crime rates stabilized after 2002; violent crime rates declined for both males and females since 1994; firearm-related crime has plummeted since 1993. From www.ojp.usdoj.gov/bsj/glance.htm#Crime.

CHAPTER 12

If It's Going to Be, It Starts With Me

"My cooperation with God's operation leads to a Jesus revelation."

—Ed Delph

Fred was a peace-at-all-costs kind of guy. He hated conflict and steered clear whenever he could. At college, he met Patty, who would eventually become his wife. They dated and had fun together; it seemed like a match made in Heaven. Little did they know that a few years later their marriage would be like hell on earth.

The first three years were wonderful. Both of them worked. They traveled and enjoyed a carefree lifestyle. Then the children started coming. The firstborn, little Emma, created the most difficult adjustment. Patty's attention was divided and she doted on the baby. Her hormonal changes threw her emotions into a tailspin. Plus, she was tired all the time, and she lost her desire for sex. Fred's irritation and resentment of the situation grew, but, not wanting to make waves, he kept his feelings to himself. Patty thought everything was OK and that the marriage was on an even keel—except when there was a blowup and Fred would retreat to his "cave" and not talk.

Eventually Fred became infatuated with Daphne, a coworker who caused his skin to crawl with desire. He found that she talked with him, not like Patty. She would listen and accept him for who he was and was not critical—so unlike Patty. The affair began with "harmless" joking at work, followed by private conversations, e-mails, and phone calls. Eventually Fred purchased a separate cell phone just to handle his conversations with Daphne. After all, he didn't want to hurt Patty's feelings by her discovering all these calls on their shared cell phone bill.

These conversations led to going out for coffee, then lunch, then a hotel. And just like the "young man lacking sense" in Proverbs 7, Fred went "like an ox to the slaughter" into the consummation of his passions.

In that brief encounter, Fred betrayed his Christian values, wife, kids, all that he held dear and all that others envied about their seemingly ideal family. Yet Fred felt exhilarated. His lust was satisfied and for the moment he felt justified in his extramarital tryst. Soon Fred began feeling guilty, but he couldn't break off his affair with Daphne, who was becoming increasingly demanding of his attention. He was hooked by his lust. He hardened himself to his feelings of guilt, and kept up the guise of the attentive husband and father at home—until Patty found an e-mail and Fred had to come clean with his deed.

"How could you do this to me and the children?" she demanded. "I've been faithful to you all these years"...and on and on. Or so it seemed to Fred. Hadn't he apologized to her and sincerely promised never to do it again? He realized that she was devastated, and clearly he was at fault. He knew that he deserved her initial outbursts of grief, shock, and anger, and he felt like a lout when he saw her tears flowing.

But then her anger came, sometimes cold and steely, sometimes accompanied by sarcasm and barbed darts aimed at his manhood, puncturing his promises to be a better husband and father than ever before. Other times she would fly into a rage over what he considered to be minor infractions of her rules for him: failing to drop off the kids at their music lessons, forgetting to pick up the dry cleaning, or—absolutely the worst—not calling when he was going to be late getting home from the office. Even his most sincere expressions of gratitude or appreciation or praise for her were met with a snort of disapproval.

They saw a marriage counselor, but the trust—well, that was not quite restored. A year went by, then two. Why wasn't Patty getting over this stuff? After all, in Fred's estimation, he was a changed man.

Every time a TV show or movie depicted unfaithfulness, Patty was hit afresh with the hurt and rejection from Fred's unfaithfulness. Bracing herself against the shock of pain, she protected herself the only way she knew how—with anger. Fred would see Patty's look of disdain and feel the emotional daggers. "How will we ever deal with this?" they both wondered. "How will we get our trust and marriage back?"

Unfortunately, this scene plays out in my (Alan's) counseling room more than I would like to admit. Trust is shattered into a million pieces like a China vase dropped to the floor, and I am asked, "Can you put us back together again?"

"No, I cannot. But I know the One who can," I say.

How Can I Begin to Trust Other People Again?

How can you trust in other people? The answer is simple: You can't. As the preceding chapter enumerates, God's Word declares that you are not to put your trust in other people. Paradoxically, however, there is a way that you can effectively trust in others.

In the classic devotional, *My Utmost for His Highest*, Oswald Chambers wrote:

"Put God First in Trust."

Jesus did not commit Himself unto them...for He knew what was in man (John 2:24-25).

Our Lord trusted no man; yet He was never suspicious, never bitter, never in despair about any man, because He put God first in trust; He trusted absolutely in what God's grace could do for any man. If I put my trust in human beings first, I will end in despairing of everyone; I will become bitter, because I have insisted on man being what no man ever can be—absolutely right. Never trust anything but the grace of God in yourself or in anyone else.[1]

Although the Bible says that Jesus put His trust in no man, in a way He *did* put His trust in the disciples. He left these handpicked men and women with the job of preaching the Kingdom of God to the entire world. How could He do this knowing how untrustworthy people are? On the one hand, He was able to trust because of His faith in the Father's plan. But on the human level, the key was this: He gave his disciples the Holy Spirit.

Acts 1:4,8 (NIV) describes this phenomenon, which occurred following Jesus' resurrection from the dead:

On one occasion, while He was eating with them, He gave them this command: "Do not leave Jerusalem, but wait for the gift My Father promised, which you have heard Me speak about....But you will receive power when the Holy Spirit comes on you; and you will be My witnesses in Jerusalem, and in all Judea and Samaria, and to the ends of the earth."

Notice this: Jesus did not want them to do anything until they had the gift of the Holy Spirit. The disciples obeyed Him and stayed in Jerusalem praying. Of course, He made it difficult for them to leave, too, given the fear factor of the crowds—who had just crucified their Lord—on the streets below the upper room where the disciples were all huddled. *Jesus didn't trust them until they had received the gift of the Spirit.* The Spirit is the only way we can love the way Jesus loved and trust others the way Jesus trusted His disciples.

The apostle Paul gives us more insight into the work of the Holy Spirit in a person's life when he writes to the Galatian church, *"My dear children, for whom I am again in the pains of childbirth until Christ is formed in you"* (Gal. 4:19 NIV). The Galatians were committed followers of Christ. But some teachers (called Judaizers) were insisting that they needed to follow the Old Testament Jewish laws in order to be righteous. So Paul felt as if he were giving birth to their faith a second time, backtracking to their starting point to return them to their freedom from sin in Christ. Having been set free from sin by faith in Christ, they were now trying to earn God's continuing favor by keeping Old Testament law—the very law whose rigorous demands were satisfied by Jesus' death on the Cross.

They were trying to do in the flesh—by their "good" deeds— what could only be accomplished in the power of the Spirit. Paul continued in Galatians 5:16 to say that if we walk by the Spirit, we will not carry out the desires of the flesh. Therefore, we won't participate in the things our flesh wants to do, such as immorality, impurity, sensuality, and so forth. The complete list is found in verses 19 through 21, and it ain't pretty.[2] But following that gruesome recitation is another list: the sweet fruit of the Spirit, which brings such pleasure to God. The love-joy-peace-patience-kindness list.

Jesus doesn't give us commandments without empowering us to do them. We might think we can't live according to God's standard because He expects too much of us, when, in actuality, the problem lies within ourselves. We cannot do the things He wants us to do in our own strength. The fruit of the Spirit cannot occur unless Someone greater than ourselves counteracts our selfish wills and desires. The catalyst for the growth of that fruit is the Holy Spirit. That is why Jesus told His disciples to wait in Jerusalem. He knew that unless they were filled with the Spirit, they would surely fail in their mission.

The Spirit is with us not only to convict us of sin, but also to empower us to be and to do the things Jesus says we are to be and to do. In First Corinthians 13:4-7, the apostle Paul lists the characteristics of perfect love. This love is patient, kind, not envious, not boastful, not proud, not rude, not self-seeking, not easily angered; it keeps no record of wrongs and doesn't delight in evil, but rejoices with the truth. Love "always protects, always trusts, always hopes, always perseveres."

Now let's be honest—how many of us can actually love someone else that way consistently? Not just on a good day, not just when they're being especially nice to us, not just when we don't have any job pressures or PMS issues, but every day—day in and day out.

And do you see all the things that love is "not"? Envious, boastful, proud, rude—when was the last time you got through a day without exhibiting any of those characteristics? We mean deep down inside in your heart of hearts. Can you honestly watch an hour of commercial-laden television or flip through a magazine that survives on advertising without feeling that you're somehow "less than..."?

OK, so what's the point? That you're a lost unregenerate soul, and you might as well give up, because you'll never be good enough for God? Ha! There's a self-defeating deception straight from the liar himself. Of course not! God knows our hearts. He knows what selfishness inherently resides within us. That's why He sent us a Savior to pay the price for our imperfections with His own perfect, sinless blood.

But God also wants us to know that He didn't just atone for our sins then leave us here on earth to struggle along as best we can, trying to live up to His impossible expectations for us. No, rather Paul tells us in Philippians 1:6 that we can be confident that God not only began a life-changing work in us with Jesus' death on the Cross, but He is also faithfully carrying it through to completion. He is at work in each of us as individuals and in the church as an institution to make us a perfect whole.

So, how does this Fruit-of-the-Spirit stuff relate to trusting in other people in relationships, marriage, or ministry? The answer is easy (living it out is the hard part): Trust in the Lord to work in them and in you. If, as He says in Philippians, the life of Christ is being formed in a person, you have the assurance that God Himself will complete His work of spiritual formation. Even if a person has wounded or betrayed you, you should be able to trust the work of God in that person's life. It is not the person you trust, but God doing His work. No matter how far gone that person or that relationship may seem to you, you are assured that *"with God all things are possible"* (Matt. 19:26).

Achieving Oneness and Building Trust

Such hope is an outstretched hand to a couple like Patty and Fred, who have gone over the cliff of betrayal. God's very character of trust gives them hope that they can move beyond their fears, rejection, abandonment, bitterness, and selfishness. If you find yourself in that desperate place, know that His hand is extended to you, too.

Others who have gone before you have learned to forgive and trust again. But it takes time and the willingness to be honest and deal with the attitudes and little dishonesties that led to your fractured relationship. You must look back and honestly assess what each of you sowed—even years ago—that sprouted and grew into your harvest of pain. Each of you probably, unwittingly, carried little seedlings from the past into your relationship. The fruit of many types of sin doesn't appear until years later.

Other seeds of destruction to trust are lack of a virile devotional time with God, lack of understanding how to walk in His Spirit, and the inability to choose truth over emotion.

The following diagram illustrates how two people achieve "oneness" in a relationship. You will observe that no matter how much individuals desire such oneness, invariably conflicts arise between them. These principles apply to all types of relationships: from friendship, to familial, to romantic, to marital. As you will see, trust can be lost at crucial points along the way.

The Relationship Cycle[3]

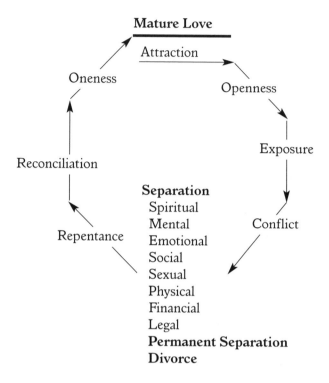

Looking at the diagram, let's walk through the development of Mandy and Ray's relationship. (Remember them from Chapter 2?) They met when Mandy, a pharmaceutical representative, dropped by Ray's dermatology clinic to display her company's latest products. Perky, bright-eyed, and friendly, she immediately caught Ray's eye. Mandy was thrilled when he, several years her senior, asked her to dinner. She liked his air of confidence and the respect he commanded among his staff at the clinic. Their initial *attraction* led to several dates.

Mandy felt safe with him; he reminded her of the stable father she'd always wished she'd had. She easily opened up with him and shared her life story. Ray was a good listener, and they shared many common interests: old movies, modern art, golden retrievers, long walks in the park, even a weakness for rocky road ice cream.

Ray was drawn to a certain little-girl vulnerability that endeared Mandy to him. He was impressed with her quick wit and attentiveness (he liked the way she was built, too), and conversing with her felt natural and easy. He found himself opening up to her in ways he never had with any other woman. Mandy and Ray were in the thralls of the *openness* stage. Some call it infatuation.

As Christians, they battled their powerful physical attraction for each other, striving—though not always succeeding—to maintain a godly moral standard. Realizing they had reached a point of commitment, they decided to get married. Yet even before they "tied the knot," certain irritating attitudes and behaviors were *exposed* in each other. Within days following their wedding, Mandy developed dark circles under her eyes because Ray's snoring kept her awake at night. She had not been prepared for how powerful his sexual drive would be. He left the toilet seat up. And he never balanced his checkbook.

After the initial passion of their honeymoon, Mandy preferred sleep to sex. When she did "get the urge," it was often in mid-afternoon, while Ray was working. She and Ray seemed to keep time on opposite biological clocks. He'd had no idea how long it took her to put on her makeup in the morning. But, as "good Christians," Mandy and Ray didn't say anything to each other about these annoyances—at least, not at first.

Before long, however, these irritants led to *conflict*. Their first argument scared them both. Ray yelled at Mandy, who burst into tears. Ray perceived her tears as manipulation and stormed out of the room, slamming the door behind him. Mandy, having witnessed similar scenes between her mother and all her "daddies," felt choking fear that her marriage was over. This *separation* was only temporary, of course, and Ray soon returned with a bouquet of flowers and apologies for losing his temper.

They kissed and made up, but the damage was done. Mandy's trust in Ray as her father figure began to fray. Over the course of their marriage, such scenes played out again and again. Every time Ray walked out, Mandy's fragile sense of security in their relationship unraveled a bit more. She was sure that one of these times, he was simply not going to return. What she didn't realize was that Ray's greatest fear was that he would lose control of his temper and cause physical harm to his precious wife. So he left in those situations in order to regain his composure.

Meanwhile, the emotional distance between them developed into a chasm. They no longer prayed together, so their separation affected them spiritually as well as physically, sexually, and socially. Because Mandy didn't trust the way Ray handled finances, she separated their checking accounts as well. They were basically leading separate lives long before she asked him to move out.

Fortunately for Ray and Mandy (and their children), they sought guidance from a biblically based counselor who helped them each to see their contributions to the disruptions in their relationship. Mandy recognized how she brought hurts from her past daddies' failures into her marriage, and then judged Ray according to their unfaithfulness to her and her mother. Ray, meanwhile, saw how much his outbursts of anger and abrupt exits struck at the heart of Mandy's fear of abandonment. Their counselor guided them through steps of asking and extending forgiveness, then *repenting* for their actions.

Both of them realized that their focus had been on themselves and their hurts while judging the other person's failures. This judgment didn't allow room for the other partner to change, even if he or she wanted to. Moreover, they understood that judging each other was sinful, placing themselves on the throne of Almighty God, as though they were without fault or sin. As Mandy and Ray walked through the process of asking for forgiveness and reconciling with each other, they learned to repent of their sins toward each other (and toward God).

Mandy and Ray came out of their sessions with their counselor with more understanding of each other than they'd had earlier in their relationship. They could see each other more realistically and accept the other's human shortcomings, knowing that they had a few of their own. As they learned to agree with God about their own failures and sinful behaviors, as they walked through the process of forgiving and reconciling with each other, Mandy and Ray experienced new levels of *oneness* than ever before in their relationship. Recognizing that this process would probably repeat itself throughout the course of their marriage, they began to extend godly grace toward each other and soon found themselves on the road to *mature love.*

So How Does This Process Apply to You?

God has intended for relationships to reach mature love, but most of us bail out in the conflict stage, "ping-ponging" from relationship to relationship. The main problem is that we have developed inappropriate strategies of either attacking the other person or withdrawing at the first sign of conflict because we trust in ourselves (which we are doing even if we say we can't trust). You can be your own worst enemy in relationships.

By choosing to work through conflicts together instead of escalating or running away from them, two persons can continue to nurture their relationship toward mature love. Once past the conflict episode, those who choose to work through the process may move through the phases of repentance, reconciliation, and oneness on to mature love. You may notice that a relationship can continue to grow each time a new conflict episode arises, moving to deeper and deeper levels of mature love. This is what makes a successful relationship.

As a pastor, I (Ed) have noticed a similar process in people trying to find a church where they feel comfortable attending. They may visit a church and decide they like it (attraction) and begin attending services. Soon they get to know the people and history of the congregation better (openness and exposure), even to the point of seeing some of the problems that every social group has. At this point, conflict often ensues. Many people opt to leave and try another church, but some will stay and try to resolve the conflict. Once reconciliation occurs, they bond with the people with whom they've successfully negotiated a resolution (oneness). After several times through this cycle, they no longer even think of leaving for another church (mature view of church membership).

You Can't Trust Other People Until You Trust God

This process of trusting in God's grace at work in another person is impossible if you don't trust God. First, develop your own trust in God; then you will be able to trust Him in other people. Remember that your faith in God upholds your trust. In order to build that faith, you must know God and His Word. Knowing Him builds your faith, which bolsters your trust and helps you develop your own vision of trust.

Keep in mind that when you trust in people, you will be disappointed from time to time. We all know that nobody is perfect, yet we place our trust in others expecting them to be righteous, true, merciful, and sensitive. Do you believe that anybody can live up to this standard at all times? Not only can no one meet that standard, but most of us don't even come close. Most of us will never live up to the expectations of some individuals. Your vision of trust will allow you to look down the forks in the road of trust and make it possible for you to choose to trust again.

Intelligent Trust

You must practice forgiveness toward others in order to get past the hurt of being let down. Remember to trust not in the person but in God's Holy Spirit at work in his or her life.

If you ever feel that God has let you down in some way, stop and take a look at the big picture. *God will never let you down.*

When Alan was in high school, he was greatly influenced by a fellow gymnast named Doug, who competed in gymnastics for Springfield College in Massachusetts. Throughout his high school years, Alan often took the train to Springfield from his home in New York to work out in the gym with Doug. They also spent hours talking about life and philosophy, and Alan looked forward to high school graduation, so he could compete for Springfield College, too. But when Alan arrived for his freshman year, he felt deserted by Doug, who had graduated and moved away. Another friend, Mike, tried to comfort Alan and help him understand

God's love for him expressed through the sacrifice of His Son, Jesus. Finally, Mike said, "Alan, people will always let you down. But God will never let you down. Who knows what's best for you—an infinite God or a finite you?"

Mike's words made such an impression that two hours later, Alan bowed his head and prayed to ask the Lord to come into his life. For the next two years, Alan counted Mike as his closest friend and often went to him for spiritual counsel. So it's no surprise that when Alan and Pauly got married, Mike was Alan's best man. Within a couple of years, however, Alan began seeing changes in Mike. His business began consuming his time and energy. His church attendance became irregular. He became critical of his wife and began giving too much attention to his secretary, a seductive divorcée. Eventually Mike lost both his marriage and his business. And Alan could not help but remember Mike's words, "People will always let you down."

If Alan's faith in God were based solely on the word of Mike, certainly his faith in God would have been shaken. But by this point in his spiritual journey, Alan trusted the Word of God. He knew that "God will never let you down," not merely because Mike had said so. But he had read of God's faithfulness in the Bible and had seen God's faithfulness at work in answer to his prayers.

The liar will try to persuade you that God has let you down and therefore is not worthy of trust. But remember his Anti-Trust Strategy and that the liar is always a liar. It is his very nature, just as God's very nature is Truth. If you think that God has let you down, then you are overlooking an important factor in that particular situation. Examine yourself. Examine your thinking. What are your motives? What does God's Word say about the situation? Have faith in God's Word. *Have faith in God!*

The ability to trust is yours. Do not lose it.

Choose to trust!

ENDNOTES

1. Oswald Chambers, *My Utmost for His Highest* (New York, Dodd, Mead, and Company, 1935, Fifty-first printing), 152.

2. Galatians 5:19-21 (NIV) reads, *"Now the deeds of the flesh are evident, which are: immorality, impurity, sensuality, idolatry, sorcery, enmities, strife, jealousy, outbursts of anger, disputes, dissensions, factions, envying, drunkenness, carousing, and things like these, of which I forewarn you, just as I have forewarned you, that those who practice such things will not inherit the kingdom of God."*

3. This chart was developed by Victorious Christian Living International and is used by permission.

CHAPTER 13

In God We Trust?

"God is getting you ready for what He has ready for you."

—Pastor Joseph Garlington

◆·▸◉◂·◆

Where Did You Lose Your Trust?

Before you can trust God, you must be able to ignore the influences of our culture, demolish the idol of self-reliance, and replace trust-destroying vows with vows that help you to trust. You cannot make a new law without rescinding the old one—otherwise the old one is still in effect. Likewise, you cannot effectively choose to trust God and His grace in others if you still have vows in your heart that you will never trust anyone. You must identify those judgments and vows. You must weigh them against the Word of God and your wisdom as a mature adult. (Remember, most of those vows were made in your youth.) Finally, you must renounce them and ask God to break their power over your life.

This process requires the work of the Holy Spirit. Often we cannot remember the initial traumatic incidents, resulting judgments, and vows. The Holy Spirit must bring them to our remembrance through prayer.

Pauly's Story

This chapter title (*In God We Trust?*) assumes that somewhere along the way you initially trusted God, and then lost that trust. But maybe you have never trusted Him in the first place and are wondering what we're talking about. Maybe you've gone to church religiously, or maybe you've occasionally visited at Christmas and Easter. Maybe you've questioned what all the Jesus hoopla is about. Or maybe you think you've done just fine without Him.

But now...there must be *some* reason you've decided to read a book on the subject of trust. So how does a person begin that initial walk of trust with the Lord? We'll use Pauly's story as an example:

Pauly grew up in a secure, loving family in southwestern Pennsylvania. Her family happened to be Jewish, and they frequently socialized at their local Jewish Community Center. Developed on a former coal baron's estate, the Center's three-story manor house, picnic grounds, swimming pools, tennis courts, and playground formed the idyllic setting for most of her family's leisure activities. And, utilized almost exclusively by members of the close-knit Jewish community, it also represented a place of great safety, where kids could run around and play, and their parents didn't have to worry about what they were getting into.

However—ah, you knew there would be a "however," didn't you—that safety wasn't 100 percent assured. When Pauly was about eight years old, the Center hired a caretaker named "Red," who took a liking to the young girls. Red often invited Pauly to come sit on his lap as she was playing outside. His breath smelled sweet—although Pauly didn't know then that the smell was from whiskey. Sometimes he would take her hand and put it on a lump in his pants. She didn't know what it was.

Red bided his time and one day invited little Pauly to meet him upstairs on the third floor of the Center manor house. That area wasn't used very often and it was dark and cool and dusty. We won't go into all the details of what happened there. Fortunately for Pauly, it didn't include penetration, but it gave her much more of an education than she was ready for at the time. And it left her with a too-soon awakened sexuality and an abiding sense of guilt. Like so many child molesters, Red told her, "Don't tell anyone. This is our secret."

A few days later, Pauly's mother mentioned that Red had been fired for peeping through the girls' locker room windows. "He's never done anything to you, has he?" her mom asked. Pauly felt cold prickles of shame and shook her head no.

Why did she say no? Was she afraid of punishment? Pauly is 55 years old today, but she still isn't quite sure. What she does know is that innocence was lost. Trust was broken. Guilt and shame engulfed her. She'd disappointed her mother (her idol). But she couldn't go back and undo her participation in that dark secret event in the third floor shadows of the Jewish Community Center.

Some of you have undergone much more trauma than that in your lives. Some women have been sexually abused over and over again. Some children are repeatedly beaten or verbally and emotionally abused by out-of-control parents or stepparents or baby-sitters. People who are supposed to be protectors have been perpetrators. And if you can't trust them, then who can you trust?

Pauly wasn't consciously aware that her trust was broken. She just knew that she never again felt comfortable discussing sexual issues or her deepest feelings with her mother. Playing spin the bottle at junior high parties shamed and embarrassed her, but she never told her mom. ("How was the party, Pauly?" "Fine.") And when she lost her virginity against her will to a drunken high school boyfriend, she hid that secret from her mother, as well.

Loss of virginity led to promiscuity. One cigarette led to chain-smoking. One night of drinking whiskey sours led to four college years of boozing and pot smoking. How she managed to compete in gymnastics and graduate *magna cum laude,* she cannot say. But it was at great expense to her mental and emotional health, and she developed painful outbreaks of acne.

Back home after graduation, she tried to maintain the façade of a clean-cut scholar-athlete, while trying to figure out how to smoke pot in her bedroom without her parents finding out. She felt like a hypocrite, hiding her despair and shame from them, desperately needing their love and approval, yet fearing their loss if her parents learned the truth. Eventually she landed a job teaching gymnastics in another town while she tried to pull her life together.

She lived with her boss, Ed, and his wife, BG, at their home on the site of their gymnastics camp nestled in a valley among Amish farms in central Pennsylvania. They had no television or radio reception—this was prior to the days of cable and satellite TV. So the members of their household, a mix of family members and gymnasts training at their facility, would sit around the kitchen table and talk in the evenings. It seemed to Pauly that no matter what topic began the conversation, eventually it would turn to spiritual matters.

BG, a talented artist and photographer, had a carefree, easygoing personality. She had not given spiritual matters much thought until just a few months prior to Pauly's arrival at the camp. Then, on an early morning photo shoot out in the meadows near her home, an older gentleman rode up to her on a bicycle and said, "The Lord sent me to you." Astonished and curious, BG listened to the man's Gospel message and decided it was true. So in a simple act of faith, she invited Jesus into her life and became His messenger herself.

So what was this message? Pauly was intrigued by BG's loving perseverance in telling her guests—despite their insistence that she had lost a good bit of her intellect—that Jesus was alive, that He had died for them and come back from the dead, and that He loved them.

It was a simple message, yet difficult for Pauly to comprehend. Perhaps because of her Jewish upbringing and a centuries-old mistrust of so-called Christians who persecuted her ancestors. Perhaps because of her fear that her mother would never speak to her again if she joined the "enemy" side. Perhaps because she had a head full of the liar's accusations: "You're no good." "You're too far gone." "Why should God care about you?" "You need to clean up your act before He'll even listen to you." "You think He'd let you off the hook that easily?" "You think He'd give you something for nothing?"

She decided to read through the Bible and started at the beginning in the Book of Genesis. But when she got to the third book, Leviticus, she was stopped in her tracks by verse 17 of chapter 5. It said, *"Now if a person sins and does any of the things which the Lord has commanded not to be done, though he was unaware, still he is guilty, and shall bear his punishment."* Ignorance of God's Law was no excuse! Now she knew she was going to hell.

She spent sleepless nights trying to pray ("God, are You there?"), yet feeling as though her prayers bounced off the tin ceilings of the farmhouse and slapped her in the face in reproach for her insolence. Could she trust the New Testament portion of the Bible that BG referred to constantly? How could she know for certain that it was true? Could she trust God to handle the consequences of the rejection she was sure would come if she "became a Christian"?

There was no way to know the answers to all her doubting questions prior to making a decision. But she wanted to be so sure. Whom could she trust? BG? Well, BG was nice and loving and kind and had an attractive quality that Pauly desired, but...

The accusations inside her head? Those had become increasingly intense and noisy, yet for the first time in her life, she'd begun to question them, to try arguing against them. She did not yet know that they originated from the liar.

Her mother? She knew she'd let her mother down in so many ways over the years and there was no way to go back and undo those events. Then, with sudden clarity, Pauly "saw" herself standing before the throne of God at the end of her life and realized that she was there alone. Her mother was not with her. She would not be able to point to her mother and say, "Well, God, I couldn't accept Your Son as my Savior because of my mother here."

Ultimately, she decided that the only person in the entire universe she could trust was God Himself. If He was there and He was real and He was all the Bible said He was, then she could trust Him to hear her prayers and answer her and reveal Himself to her in a tangible way. So she would call out to Him with all the faith and belief she could muster. She would talk to Him, believing that He was there and He was hearing her. And if nothing happened, well then, she would take it from there. But she was going for it. She had everything to gain and nothing to lose.

She was driving in her car down a starlit, two-lane stretch of Route 45 around 9:30 p.m. when she started talking to God. "God," she began, "You know I'm Jewish. I don't want to not be Jewish. But I do want to know You. And I want You to forgive my sins. And if Jesus is really the promised Messiah for Your Jewish people, and You want me to accept Him as my Messiah so that my sins can be forgiven, then I want to do that. I don't want to do anything You don't want me to do, so if Jesus isn't the Messiah, then I want You to show me that, too. But if He is, then, Lord, I want to accept the price He paid for my sins with His blood, and I want to receive Him into my life. Take me, I'm Yours."

Does that sound like trust to you? Pauly thinks it must have sounded like trust to God, too, because she had an immediate response from Him.

An overwhelming sense of peace flooded her entire being. She suddenly noticed the crystal-clear, starry sky. She became aware that all the noise and the accusing voices inside her head had been silenced. And she thought, *This must be peace of mind.*

That was the beginning of what has now been a 33-year walk of trust in the Lord for Pauly. Over the years, she's experienced her ups and downs like any normal person. She's had her moments of being angry with God, of not wanting to accept the way things were going with her life, her marriage, her relationships, her kids, her finances. But through it all, she has never lost her basic trust in the Lord, her belief that yes, He is there and He is real and He is who His Word says He is.

How about you?

Forgiveness Makes the Future Possible

Before the power of a vow can be broken, you must invoke the power of God in your own heart. *You must forgive the person who hurt you.*

Just as God forgave you for your sins and all the times you let Him down, you must forgive others. Just as God is willing to give you another chance by working His life in you, you must give others, in whom the life of Christ is manifested, the opportunity to show themselves trustworthy to you.

Develop a lifestyle of forgiveness. Forgive those who have hurt you and led you to make vows against trust. Forgive also those who have hurt your loved ones, when you have taken offense on behalf of others. This can be the most difficult type of forgiveness. Ask the Holy Spirit's help in prayer.

Forgiveness can be difficult. There are many good books available to help you forgive and restore relationships with those who have hurt you.[1] If you are having trouble in this area, we urge you to read, study your Bible, and ask for God's help in forgiving others.

Hanging on the Cross, dying as punishment for crimes He had not committed, Jesus said, *"Father, forgive them; for they do not know what they are doing"* (Luke 23:34). Jesus knew that the Jews and Roman soldiers who were crucifying Him did not see the "big picture." They thought they were putting to death a blasphemer and a traitor to Caesar, as they had many times before. Clearly, they did not understand who Jesus was and the significance of their act.

Similarly, many of those who have hurt you do not fully understand the ramifications of their acts. They don't realize that their purposeful or insensitive action will cause you to lose your ability to trust. They do not realize that you are a child of God. They just don't see the big picture. Forgive them, as Jesus did. You are the one held in the bondage of unforgiveness.

Richard had borrowed a huge sum of money from his boss, Sam. He'd invested it in Enron stock. When Enron went under, Richard lost his house, his car, and his marriage. Finally he went to Sam, sobbing, and told him he couldn't pay back the loan. Sam, a generous man, forgave Richard the entire debt. But later, Sam heard that Richard, who owned a small rental house, had evicted a tenant for missing one month's rent. What do you think Sam did?

Actually Jesus told this story in Matthew 18, in which "Richard" is the servant of an unnamed man. Here's the conclusion of the story:

> Then the master called the servant in. "You wicked servant," he said, "I canceled all that debt of yours because you begged me to. Shouldn't you have had mercy on your fellow servant just as I had on you?" In anger his master turned him over to the jailers to be tortured, until he should pay back all he owed. This is how My heavenly Father will treat each of you unless you forgive your brother from your heart (Matthew 18:32-35 NIV).

Forgiveness is not an option in the Kingdom of God. It is the command of our Lord.

Sally's Story

Sally and Bill were married with two precious daughters. Bill's job seemed to provide an adequate income and a lovely home in a new subdivision. They went to church and Sunday school class every week. They looked like the typical, upwardly mobile American family.

But beneath the surface, things were not right. The communication between them lacked intimacy. At home, Bill would sit in front of the TV and "vege." Sally was busy with their daughters, dancing lessons, her Bible study and girlfriends.

Bill came from a working-class background and could not lose the "poor man's" mentality. He felt pressured to maintain a successful appearance but never felt as if he measured up to Sally's expectations. When he got a potentially lucrative job, he could not perform. This was also true in the bedroom, where not much would happen month after month, year after year. Sally thought something was wrong but blamed herself. Maybe after having two kids and losing her shape, she was not as desirable anymore. Or maybe she was just not as pleasing to him.

At this point, they came to me (Alan) for counsel. We began making progress, but as we homed in on some of Bill's issues, he suddenly switched from open transparency to closed defensiveness. After one particularly intense session, he withdrew from counseling and refused to return.

Over the years, Sally and Bill were hounded with money problems. Creditors started to call and Sally did not understand it. She would refer them to Bill, but he said he paid them all and she should not worry. One day, while she was watering the houseplants, she heard a knock on the door. She opened it to two men in business suits who asked, "Are you Mrs. Smith?" She said yes.

"We are serving you with a foreclosure notice—you have not paid your mortgage in more than a year."

Sally was shocked. Disbelieving thoughts raced through her head. *He said he took care of it. He said to just give him time and it would all work out.* Sally felt betrayed, used, and rejected. This was the final straw. She had put up with Bill's irresponsibility and lies and deceit long enough. Her girls were practically grown, and he was hardly a father they could respect. Now he wasn't even providing for their most basic needs. She called a lawyer and acted on the promise that she had made to herself for many years, but this time she would follow through. She would divorce him and never have to put up with this kind of nonsense again.

Then the thoughts came. *How could I have been such a fool? How could I have trusted him when I knew he was doing pornography and he would never give me the money I needed to run the house? I would borrow from my parents but I knew something was wrong.*

I see many such people in my counseling practice. Some of them never get over this type of anger. They're caged. They wonder, *Why did I have to end up paying the price for someone else's misdeeds?*

They tend to explode, blaming their partner, their boss, their job, but not taking responsibility for their own actions. Or they implode, becoming withdrawn and depressed, rehearsing the past and what they didn't do or should have done. They "beat themselves up" for their failures of the past. They may seek help, but first they try to handle it themselves. However, it's hard to be objective about some-one so close who has hurt them so deeply. They try to pray, but their prayers seem ineffective. Finally they realize that they need to talk to somebody. But the liar whispers to them that their failures are so shameful and unforgivable that they must not tell anyone, not even their counselor.

If they don't seek help, they keep rehearsing the pain of the hurt over and over again. They get stuck, creating mental scenarios of what they think could have or should have been. On a day-to-day level, they keep functioning. Their habits of spiritual discipline go by the wayside, and they live and make decisions according to the flesh.

They may try to anesthetize their pain through drugs, sex, work, projects, hobbies, relationships. They become obsessive in trying to get away from their pain. Yet they kick themselves repeatedly. In their gut they know one thing, but their mind is telling them some-thing else. They want to be "good Christians" and not lash out at the other person, yet inside they have "murder" in their heart. This cre-ates tremendous tension, because they believe that a good Christian would just forgive and forget and walk away from the hurt and pain.

They blame themselves, yet deep inside they know it wasn't en-tirely their fault. They swing crazily between totally blaming the other person and totally blaming themselves. They're far from God, but they may not even realize it because they've begun substituting something else—an idol, so to speak—in His place. They're lost.

Also during this time, they tell their story to their friends and get so much conflicting advice that they're tossed to and fro emotionally. They don't know who to believe or what to think. Their hurt gives them a jaundiced eye in telling their story to begin with.

They can't trust their own perceptions or the counsel of their well-meaning friends. They can no longer trust the one who betrayed them. And, feeling as though He has let them down, they can't trust God.

After an ugly divorce filled with haggling over details, Sally and her daughters moved in with her parents. She was left financially and emotionally destitute. During the proceedings, Bill had undergone a Dr. Jekyll-to-Mr. Hyde transformation. At first, he played "Mr. Nice Guy" and proposed that they settle their differences out of court. But when Sally hired a lawyer to protect an inheritance, Bill one-upped her. His attorney used emotionally manipulative ploys, confused the issues, and drew out the legal proceedings by showing up late for meetings or canceling at the last minute.

Meanwhile, Bill used his visitation times to poison his daughters' attitudes toward their mother. And he pitted the girls against each other, showing extreme favoritism toward the younger one. Sally dealt with her pain and hurt and the feeling of being used. Both girls would return from their weekends with their dad in tears.

Unable to afford professional counseling, Sally sought advice from her friends and tried to trust the only one she could: the Lord. She threw herself into a new job, her Bible, and the women who supported her through her ordeal.

Over the course of a year, Sally gradually returned to a place of peace and safety as she lived out the Truth that she knew. She spent time in a quiet corner of her bedroom each day, praying and reading her Bible. She wrote in her journal a list of all the things that God's Word said were true about her. She made lists of His promises to her. When He brought to mind the names of people who had hurt her (including Bill), she actively took steps to forgive and reconcile with them to the best of her ability.

Gradually the bitterness and pain in her heart lifted like the morning fog off the lake outside her parents' summer home. Five years later on the shore of that lake, she married a godly man who embodied all the spiritual attributes that Bill had lacked.

ENDNOTE

1. For example: David Augsburger's *Caring Enough to Forgive* and Charles Stanley's *The Gift of Forgiveness.*

CHAPTER 14

Beginning to Trust People All Over Again

*"We are all angels with only one wing; we can
only fly while embracing each other."*

—Luciano DeCrescenzo

——————

Your interpretation of past events colors your attitudes and actions in the present. You may find yourself acting out of fear or anger, certain that your spouse, let's say, is the cause. But if that person says you're overreacting to the situation, often you'll find that your emotion is tied to a past event—something you've not worked through to the point of healing.

So how can you trust God to protect you from certain people who have wounded you terribly? What is the process of trusting in God? How do you get there from where you are? There is no formula—nothing works all the time. But it has to start with a *big* God, one bigger than your expectations, bigger than your dreams.

A God who will do as He promises far beyond all you ask or think or even imagine (see Eph. 3:20). You need a big view of God and His character—His holiness, His justice, His grace. Otherwise, you will always struggle to accept the things that come your way, that are beyond your finite ability to see only what is in front of you.

Our Western democracy affords us so many choices and so much autonomy, we easily become self-reliant. And our technology gives us a certain sense of invincibility. But the catastrophic devastation of 2005's Hurricane Katrina on the city of New Orleans demonstrated how quickly and completely the powers of nature can knock out our technology. Our government agencies were overwhelmed. Such catastrophes reveal our limitations.

So you need a big picture of God and an appropriate picture of yourself. And you need a balance between the two. If your mental focus is all about how small and awful you are, constantly confessing sin and shame, focusing on your inabilities and failures, then you will become depressed and self-centered in a negative sense. If it's all about how you can *"do all things through Christ"* (Phil. 4:13 KJV), but don't recognize your human frailties and need for His cleansing and the guidance of the Holy Spirit, you may have unrealistic expectations of what you can accomplish for Him, as opposed to what He wants to accomplish through you.

When it comes to trusting other people, your greatest need is to trust God to be working in your relationship with them. Years ago, in my (Alan's) Campus Crusade training, I learned that in order to love certain "difficult" people, we must love them "by faith." We begin our walk with God by trusting that Jesus' sacrificial death on the Cross is sufficient to cover the penalties incurred against us for our sin. We believe that truth (intellectually), then apply that truth (experientially) to ourselves by asking Jesus to be our personal Savior (faith). Faith is believing that what God says is true and acting upon it. In similar fashion, you must also live daily by faith and, at times, you'll have to love by faith.

Healthy Boundaries

John Townsend and Henry Cloud's book Boundaries introduced the concept of our need to set certain limits on how much territory within our lives we allow other people to control. For example, some mothers continue telling their adult children how to live their lives long after they've left home. Often the children of such mothers have problems saying no to their mom. Some women have never learned to say no to the sexual advances of men. They don't know how to set safe, healthy boundaries for themselves in male-female relationships.

Bridget's husband, Hugo, deserted her after a year of marriage. He went directly into an affair with another woman and rebuffed all of Bridget's attempts at counseling and reconciliation. Their divorce was finalized within six months of his leaving. However, a year later, Hugo called Bridget saying that the woman with whom he'd been living had moved away, and he was ready to pursue reconciliation with Bridget. Now Bridget's emotions are all in a jumble. Should she take Hugo back? Even though they've divorced, does God still consider him to be her husband? What should she do?

This situation is complex. There are no easy answers for Bridget. However, she needs to remain centered on God and not on Hugo. Before she can allow Hugo to reenter her life, she needs to set some boundaries for how their relationship will progress. She needs to determine whether or not she is willing to relinquish her heart again to a man who has wounded her so deeply. But whether or not she and Hugo choose to remarry, Bridget must *trust God to guide her*, rather than her emotions, or Hugo's advances, or her friends' advice.

Trusting People in Authority

Fresh out of seminary, Steven joined a Christian ministry headed by a powerful leader named Robert.[1] Through Robert's mentoring, Steven grew spiritually, vocationally, and personally. Steven believed in Robert's goals for the ministry and devoted himself to helping to make it a success. Grateful for Robert's leadership and counsel and the results he was seeing in his own life, Steven trusted him unquestioningly. But gradually he began seeing discrepancies between how Robert lived his life and certain principles from God's Word.

Steven approached Robert about these issues, but Robert rebuffed him, belittling his concerns. Steven then appealed to the ministry's board of directors, always with the hope of finding a way to work peaceably with Robert. Time and again, Robert denied any wrongdoing, accusing Steven of ingratitude, unfaithfulness to the organization, and finally, insurrection. At that point Steven realized that for his own emotional health he must set a strong emotional boundary between himself and Robert. He decided he could no longer trust Robert's abusive misuse of authority to give him unbiased counsel. He chose to leave the organization. Ultimately, he had to entrust himself to God's direction for the next step in his life.

Stella's pastor began a prison ministry, and sent her and other women from his church to minister to incarcerated men. She eventually married one of the inmates, earning his early release. He physically and emotionally abused her and her children from a previous marriage. The marriage ended in divorce.

Recent news broadcasts show us examples of police overstepping their civil authority, using racial profiling in their treatment of suspects.

God's Word tells us to obey "kings" and those "in authority" over us (1 Tim. 2:1-2). Yet Christians in Nazi Germany have been criticized for blindly complying with Hitler's anti-Semitic edicts and failing to prevent the extermination of six million Jews.

What is your responsibility, then, as a believer attempting to act in faith and obedience to God's Word? How are you to respect authorities who misuse their positions? How can you know whom to trust?

Again, we point you to God's Word. He will not violate His own principles. So if an employer asks you to cover up his embezzling, you can be sure God doesn't want you to comply. He has never re-scinded His command, *"Thou shalt not steal"* (Exod. 20:15 KJV).

The Bible contains nine letters that the apostle Paul wrote to churches, and four others he composed to church leaders. We encour-age you to read these letters and familiarize yourself with the guide-lines they contain. They are your yardstick by which you can measure the trustworthiness of your spiritual leaders. And if, as a believer in God, you cannot trust your boss at work, and you have no recourse or higher authority to whom you may appeal, then you should consider resigning. As with all other decisions in life, you must trust God to lead you to another job situation or show you how to live with a clear conscience within your current situation.

Small Steps

So on the practical side, what steps can you implement to rebuild trust in someone who has hurt you? Let's say you've gone through the "Relationship Cycle" (in Chapter 12) and have forgiven each other and reconciled. Yet you still don't feel ready to let down your guard with that person. I (Alan) think that the person has to demonstrate that he or she can be trusted. You must set your bound-aries and create a framework and then, little by little, you will see if he or she is trustworthy.

When my dad taught me to drive a car, first I sat on the passenger's side and he let me turn the key. Then one time he said, "Put your foot on the accelerator when I tell you." Next he let me sit in the driver's seat and he said, "Turn the key and push on the accelerator a little, but don't touch the gear shift."

When I'd done that successfully, he said, "Now you may take the car from here to in front of the garage, slowly, and then park it." When Dad saw that I had mastered this step with him in the passenger's seat, he let me actually pull the car into the garage.

Finally, the big day came when I was allowed to drive the car down the driveway and put it away. Wow! That seems like a long process, but I never hurt the car and I was very ready to move ahead at each stage.

This is what you will have to do in order to rebuild trust. Start small and then give the person more of a chance to be trusted. Be aware that sometimes he or she may revert to certain behaviors. But with confession, repentance, forgiveness, and reconciliation, your relationship can be restored and even greater oneness can be achieved.

Your process for restoring trust:

1. Trust God first.
2. Trust the person by faith.
3. Take small tangible steps toward rebuilding trust.

Becoming Perfect and Complete

Some people can't get past the feeling that God has dealt them a rotten blow. They blame God, the person, or the circumstances. In their picture of God, He's not big enough to handle the circumstances. Dave could not accept that after praying and having others pray for healing, his wife died from serious health problems. His version of who God is didn't provide for her death. He didn't know how to process what he perceived as God's unanswered prayer. One of my seminary professors said, "You must have a theology of suffering as well as of living." When his wife died, Dave, a devout and mature Christian, became mad at God and doubted that prayer really works. So Dave usurped the role of God because He didn't meet Dave's expectations.

Sometimes, we, like Dave, don't want to accept what God has allowed to happen. In our Western mind-set, we expect everything in our lives to be positive and new. We have trouble accepting suffering along with what we perceive as the good things in life. The Bible tells us that our trials will make us perfect (or whole and mature), complete, and lacking in nothing. We don't want to go through trials and suffering, but we still want the results.

Alexander Caron wrote: "We rejoice in the sovereignty of God because we are sure it is always exercised for the good of His people." (See Romans 8:28). We can know this to be true simply because He said it.

Psalm 13:5-6 (NIV) says *"But I trust in Your unfailing love; my heart rejoices in Your salvation. I will sing to the Lord, for He has been good to me."*

How to Claim Your Ability to Trust

Following is a sample "Judgment/Vow" table we use to help people identify the hurts, judgments, and vows that have power over their lives.

Here are the steps to using this table:

1. Ask the Holy Spirit to help you recall incidents that were critical in the loss of your ability to trust.

2. Recall a painful memory. You have probably made some judgments and a vow concerning that memory. Record that incident in abbreviated form.

3. Recall how you felt as a result of that incident. What did you conclude about it? Ask the Holy Spirit to help you to articulate the judgment that you made about the incident. What did you decide about responding to similar situations in the future? What vow was the natural result of the judgment? Ask the Holy Spirit to help you articulate the vow or vows that you made.

Here are some examples from the illustrations in this book to show you how the table works. (Important note: It is critical that you ask the Holy Spirit's help in accurately identifying the appropriate memories.) The painful incident or memory is usually the easiest to identify. Then ask yourself, *"What judgment did I make concerning that incident?"* And finally, *"What was the resulting vow?"*

Sample "Judgment/Vow" Table

This chart is a tool to help you identify and categorize the life-shaping incidents in your life. Following is a blank chart for your personal use.

INCIDENT	JUDGMENT	VOW
A cat jumps on a hot stove.	*That's hot and I don't like it.*	*I'll never jump on a stove again!*
A loud noise occurs while Albert tries to pet a white rat.	*That scares me and I don't like it.*	*I'll never try to pet any-thing white and furry again!*
Lisa's father is nice to her when he wants something.	*When men are nice it's because they are after something.*	*Always be suspicious of nice men.*
Lisa's father emotion-ally manipulates her.	*Men always try to ma-nipulate women.*	*I won't be manipu-lated.*
Lisa's father hides his business dealings from her mother.	*My father is a rascal; all men are rascals.*	*I don't trust men.*

Judgment/Vow Table

INCIDENT	JUDGMENT	VOW

Reading this book and knowing what it says can take you only so far through the process of learning to trust again. You yourself must walk through the process of forgiveness and disempower the vows that have held you in bondage. Write out your observations about your life-shaping events and lingering influences. Think about them. Understand how they affected your ability to trust God and others. (You may ask a friend, pastor, or counselor to accompany you through this process.) Then if you want to change, pray the following prayer (or something similar) as it applies to your unique situation:

Father, my Lord and my God,

I recognize how I have lost my ability to trust You due to the effects of these situations I have recorded as well as the work of the liar.

In the name of Jesus, I now demolish the idol of self-reliance. I renounce any trust I have put in myself, and from this day forward I will trust Jesus.

Forgive me, Father, for making judgments about You. Forgive me for not trusting You. Forgive me for confining You to the terms I have set up for our relationship. Help me to know You by Your Word and to begin to trust You again. Open my eyes that I might see the big picture. Help me to know You as You desire to be known.

Just as You have forgiven me of my sins, I forgive those who have hurt me. (List them by name.)

I renounce each of these vows that the Holy Spirit has shown me. Father, I ask You to break the power they have held over my life.

From this day forward I will trust You, Father, and I will trust Your grace at work in the lives of others.

Thank You for helping me to trust You again.

In the name of Your Son, Jesus Christ, I pray. Amen!

Now, like the wise man who built his house on the rock, go and be a doer of the Word. Walk the walk of faith, trusting that He who began a good work in you will be faithful to complete it.

ENDNOTE

1. Not their real names.

CONTACT THE AUTHOR

Ed Delph
Nationstrategy
7145 W. Mariposa Grande Lane
Peoria, Arizona 85383

www.nationstrategy.com
nationstrategy@cs.com

5150 N 16th St   suite B-250
Phoenix AZ 85016
E-mail- alan@walkandtalk.org
www.walkandtalk.org